Thurs.
3:30
Mid d

W9-ATP-751

The
LANGUAGE
of
DOGS

The
LANGUAGE
of
DOGS

JUSTIN SILVER

and

David Donnenfeld

GALLERY BOOKS

NEW YORK   LONDON   TORONTO   SYDNEY   NEW DELHI

G

Gallery Books
A Division of Simon & Schuster, Inc.
1230 Avenue of the Americas
New York, NY 10020

Copyright © 2014 by Justin Silver and David Donnenfeld

NOTE TO READERS: Names of some of the clients portrayed in this book have been changed. In some instances, the clients and information presented about them are composites.

All rights reserved, including the right to reproduce this book or portions thereof in any form whatsoever. For information address Gallery Books Subsidiary Rights Department, 1230 Avenue of the Americas, New York, NY 10020.

First Gallery Books hardcover edition September 2014

GALLERY BOOKS and colophon are registered trademarks of Simon & Schuster, Inc.

For information about special discounts for bulk purchases, please contact Simon & Schuster Special Sales at 1-866-506-1949 or business@simonandschuster.com

The Simon & Schuster Speakers Bureau can bring authors to your live event. For more information or to book an event contact the Simon & Schuster Speakers Bureau at 1-866-248-3049 or visit our website at www.simonspeakers.com.

Interior design by Jaime Putorti
Cover design by John Vairo Jr.
Jacket photography by Brian Friedman Photography
Interior photographs © 2014 by Brian Friedman, Heather Wines, Christian Mack, Steven Klein and Heidi Kikel.

Manufactured in the United States of America

10 9 8 7 6 5 4 3 2 1

Library of Congress Cataloging-in-Publication Data is on file.

ISBN 978-1-4767-3412-5
ISBN 978-1-4767-3414-9 (ebook)

CONTENTS

This book is dedicated to all the animals in shelters and the people who work tirelessly to save them. I'd also like to thank Laura Donnenfeld for being so caring in handling me, Dave (my co-writer and Laura's husband), and, most of all, our dogs.

INTRODUCTION

It has always been my aim to empower dog owners with the necessary tools to work effectively with and understand their beloved pets. The mission of this book is not so much to show owners what to do but to open a line of communication between dog and person. Along the way, I hope to remove some of the mystery surrounding canine behavior, in order to create and implement realistic training goals that will lead to a beautiful, long-lasting friendship.

A training session is as much a training of the owner as it is of the dog. I show an owner what to look for and encourage him or her to become more connected to the animal so that bonds may forge and grow. In many cases, there is as much time spent unlearning as there is learning. Thanks primarily to the Internet, every dog person comes equipped with information and misinformation alike.

It's been said that I "speak dog." However, I think it is more accurate to say that I "listen dog." If I have a secret, that's it, and I believe this practice is entirely underused. I also wholly believe there is no "one size fits all" approach to the training of dogs.

As an interpreter between us earthlings and these alien creatures, I often come from the point of view of the dog. In fact, I find dogs easier to understand than most people. There is more information than ever on our beloved pets, yet the gap between dogs and owners is ever widening. Worse still, new approaches to dog ownership and training are being peddled like fad diets and creating much unneeded confusion. In this book, I will endeavor to bridge this gap by focusing my attention on what matters: our four-legged kids with tails.

Speaking dog means having unspoken communication between human and animal—and it is a two-way street. We listen to the dog, and the dog listens to us. Sometimes we even agree to disagree (like when my pit bull, Pacino, seems intent on soliciting affection from every passing stranger in New York City while I am trying to walk in solitude). We compromise. As in any relationship, there are misunderstandings. When I am not understood, I try to listen and adjust my message until it *is* understood. Dogs are constantly working to convey what they're trying to say; unfortunately, we either don't listen or don't understand. New owners often have unrealistic expectations of how a dog should behave and may be surprised by even garden-variety behaviors. Dogs will bark, bite, chew, and dig, and may consider a soft welcome mat an ideal place to urinate. These tendencies will remain unchanged unless directed to more appropriate outlets. We should never wish to put a halt to the natural activities that make dogs dogs.

So how do we listen to a dog? To understand the language of

dogs, we must listen with our eyes. And we must do so in a place where we are so bombarded by stimuli that we can barely hear ourselves think. Unfortunately, as the stressors of life increase, dogs have suffered right along with us.

There is an expression: "If you stick with the basics, you never have to go back to basics." Reconnecting or connecting with a member of the canine family is about as basic and cathartic an activity as exists on God's green earth. It is primal, nourishing, and restorative for the soul. Dogs are great bellwethers for what is ailing us; sadly, they are also unintended victims of our issues du jour. Shelters are overflowing with unwanted dogs, often abandoned by those who sought "a best friend." This is nothing short of a modern-day tragedy that goes largely overlooked. Dogs cannot voice their displeasure with our decision to treat them like disposable household items; nor can they protest our unfair expectations to have them behave like something other than dogs. My business partner and co-writer, David Donnenfeld, will tell you that having a dog is "like having half a child," and I believe he's right.

Responsible pet ownership should be worn like a loose garment made of breathable fabric and not feel like a wet blanket of burden. This is not a step-by-step training manual, because no one needs one. We need guidelines, not gospel. The tagline of my dog care company (and the title of this book), *The Language of Dogs*, calls for "obedient owners and happy dogs." Although that's tongue in cheek, an owner does need to make some sacrifices in order to have a healthy, well-balanced dog. This includes things like frequent walks, regardless of the size of one's backyard. I strongly encourage owners to construct a plan that takes into account *their* dog's preferences (maybe "obedient" isn't quite so tongue in cheek after all). Children do not come with a single set of instructions, and if they did, what parent would follow them to the letter? Parents get to know their child and adjust accordingly. The same methodology should also apply to dogs. As I stated before, I believe in guidelines created by informed owners with a willingness to "speak" some dog.

CHAPTER 1

LEARNING TO SPEAK DOG

"Even the tiniest poodle or Chihuahua is still a wolf at heart."
—DOROTHY HINSHAW

Although I had a dog growing up, they did not truly become my life until I met a troubled five-month-old pit bull/border collie mix from the Bronx named Princess. She had been tossed over a fence into the small concrete yard of a house-cum-shelter that belonged to my friend Robyn. I had met Robyn some weeks earlier, when I wandered to Union Square and literally stepped on a patchwork blanket that read "Adoptable Pets." Like most New Yorkers, I was walking with my head down and looked up to find a dozen or so dogs lying on blankets in a long, happy row. Robyn immediately introduced herself and began to tell the story of each animal while fellow volunteers chimed in. Robyn is one of those people who is so genuine that you don't ask yourself, "Can she really be this upbeat?" An amiable redhead with faded freckles and a spirit that can shine on a cloudy day in Union Square, she told me, "This one was found tied to a telephone pole; this one belonged to a family who couldn't care for her anymore; this one's previous owner passed away; these puppies were found in a box on a church doorstep." Despite the fact that these dogs were in varying states of disrepair and all were homeless, Robyn shared their gut-churning stories as if they were already tales of hope and redemption.

The dogs were all super lovable, but I immediately gravitated to the pit bulls. There was nothing intimidating about these pits, as they all wore the scars and lesions of abuse and neglect. To my eyes, the stigma surrounding pit bulls made them all the more vulnerable, and who doesn't want to see an underdog triumph? I asked Robyn how to get involved. In short order I became a volunteer, and before long I was fostering dogs.

I was raised in Queens, New York, by my phenomenal single mother, and as a child I could often be found playing with our shih tzu, Zack. My mother is fond of reminding me that I would balk at going to anyone's home unless they had a dog. Dogs were always my favorite company, and that remains unchanged to this day.

Looking back, I'd say I was a normal kid. I was not particularly good in school, and, to be candid, I didn't care for it much, outside of art class. Typically, I was bored, and to deal with the boredom, I often took center stage as class clown. This behavior landed me in hot water now and again, but it also helped score me the lead in school plays. At home, my favorite activities were playing with Zack, drawing, and watching animal programs (on the one channel that aired them) with my grandfather.

My teen years were pretty normal but definitely not the "glory days" that Bruce Springsteen sang about. After high school, I attended art school in New York City, and, to this day, I feel fortunate to have studied something I still care about. After college, I stayed in Manhattan and began to find my way.

Living in New York City in my early twenties felt like a big mirage. It seemed full of opportunity, but I felt powerless to take advantage of it. With the limited resources and connections of a twentysomething from Queens, everything seemed to be just over the horizon. I wanted to get in the mix but felt stunted by the need to support myself.

I worked as a busboy in a restaurant and would hike back and forth to my mom's place at all hours. Pretty quickly, my odd hours got old for both of us, and I really needed to catch a break. That break would come when my friend Dave moved to Miami and agreed to let me sublet his place at a reduced rent. An affordable Manhattan apartment is like winning the lottery. Dave's place came with a number of amenities; it was furnished, and I knew he wouldn't care when I paid the rent. As I went through my share of low-paying jobs in the food service industry, I admittedly abused this privilege.

Within a year, the restaurant business and I parted ways, and I became a personal trainer. I loved that it was an independent, social job. This choice came as a surprise to many people who knew me growing up because I'd never been in particularly good shape. In fact, I carried some extra weight into my late teens when the bug to get fit bit with a vengeance. I became obsessive about diet and exercise. Over the course of six months, I shed some unwanted poundage and found my way into sound eating habits and a regimen of regular exercise. All of a sudden being healthy and fit made sense, so when I started personal training, I thought it was going to be an easy job. I'll readily admit it's not the most difficult job in the world, but I found it exasperating in the beginning. After I got into shape myself, I had a hard time understanding why people would not do what was necessary to get and stay healthy. My closed mentality was something I would have to move past in order to become a good trainer. Until then I just wondered why my clients—who were not only paying for a trainer but also working out at The Sports Center at Chelsea Piers, one of the country's premier fitness centers—still weren't motivated. As a trainer, I tried wearing different hats: I was the drill sergeant, the motivational speaker, the robotic rep counter, the peaceful warrior, you name it. They all produced similarly inconsistent results. Some people made progress, while others didn't. Although my clients were generally happy with my work, I was tearing my hair out in frustration. Hiring a trainer only to maintain status quo was unfathomable to me. To compound my frustrations, a few clients were regularly canceling or not showing up for appointments. As fate would have it, the client who would change my approach to personal training and ultimately help shape my philosophy on *dog* training was my most consistent no-show: an unassuming woman named Miranda.

Miranda was getting married and wanted to lose weight for her wedding. It was and still is the dream scenario for any trainer: a purposeful goal with a clear deadline. She wanted to lose twenty pounds by the big day and had ninety days to do it. Miranda was a lawyer (yes, that was her name) and the type of person who considered exercising a necessary evil at best. She never complained about it but let her feelings be known by regularly skipping our scheduled sessions. Now that her wedding date had been set, she meant business, and I went to work with renewed enthusiasm.

I designed a diet that was anything but restrictive and tailored a workout that would have me sweating as much as her. We went straight to work: tossing medicine balls back and forth, running between cones, performing plyometrics, and a world of activity-based training. Miranda bristled at anything that seemed static and boring. There would be no treadmills or traditional resistance movements, so she had no excuses. I may have been more excited than she was and made all kinds of promises to her and her fiancé.

The first week was picture-perfect. She lost six pounds and her body was coming to life. Then the second week came—she lost no weight, and her efforts in the gym were abysmal. Miranda was listless and took water breaks every two minutes, when she wasn't going to the bathroom to hide. On week three, she started showing up late and having to leave early. In week four, she didn't show up for two of her four scheduled appointments. When she weighed in after four weeks, she had gained back the six pounds she'd lost, posting a net loss of zero. I didn't know what to do and contemplated passing her along to another trainer. I decided to give it one more workout, only this time instead of participating I was going to watch her.

When she showed up, I had her do some freehand squats followed by light running in place to warm up. She pretended to squat by turning her knees inward to give the appearance of bending, which was nothing short of bizarre. I've seen people shortchange the squat to make it easier, but to this day, she is the only person I've ever seen attempt to reinvent it. It was difficult to watch, so I had her run in place. This was also tough to look at. Miranda had a strong body type and was actually in fairly good shape, but her feet did not leave the ground as she ran in place. Normally, I would have barked a little and encouraged her, but this time I did nothing and let her keep on. After a minute, she closed her eyes and kept them shut. What made that day all the more strange was, for the first time, Miranda had shown up in a genuinely good mood and said she felt great.

I let her keep running in place for a full ten minutes, which is a long time to do a little warming up. Her eyes did not open. I'm sure Miranda hoped I'd let the clock run out just like this. I told her to stop, and she told me she needed to use the restroom. When she came back, she walked with resignation toward the cones I had set up. I stopped her with a simple question: "Do you even want to get married?"

It was out of bounds, but something had to puncture her veil of denial. She wasn't getting in shape like she'd promised herself, and it was the elephant in the room. Miranda looked at me, smiled, and said, "Justin, I really don't know." I replied, "You work out like you don't," and she started to cry. Then she walked away with her face in her hands, and the reality of what I'd said started to sink in.

I've since apologized to her a thousand times for saying that, although she still thanks me for being so straight with her. For me, the comment was the culmination of many months of watching my clients (and me) fail themselves. I thought Miranda was not going to show up again, and I faced the possibility that I might be fired for making inappropriate comments. It was a dark day all the way around until . . .

Miranda came back raring to go. She explained that she didn't feel she had permission to experience the normal doubts about getting married, and it had been weighing on her. Her body language had clearly told me everything I needed to know, and as obvious as it might have been, my eyes were the ones that had been shut. From that point on, I watched people work out and always found that their efforts were commensurate with the obstacles they faced in their personal life. I became much more apt to halt a workout and ask, "What's wrong?" rather than exhort someone to push it. I practiced the art of listening with my eyes and offered my clients a bartender's ear when needed. I also watched their results improve dramatically. It was rewarding, and my client base more than tripled in the following six months.

After a few years of helping people change both their bodies and their outlook on life, it was my turn to ask, "What's wrong?" Training was fruitful, but I felt dissatisfied. It was time to do something about my life. I sensed that I needed to put myself out there and I'd been a huge fan of stand-up comedy for years. In the past I'd frequented places like the Comedy Cellar to check out the live acts of the very best. As I watched, I often wondered if I could do it myself. It was a challenge that I could not wriggle away from. Terrifying though it may be, I would have to try my hand at stand-up comedy and rather unexpectedly, it would be the decision that took me into the world of dogs.

Stand-up comedy is not an easy thing. I'd always thought I had a good sense of humor but being funny in front of an audience is far different than getting laughs when you're out with friends. To become any good at stand-up, it must be a near-daily practice. I paid my dues by passing out flyers in front of the clubs, come rain or shine. This work earns you the privilege of being onstage for five minutes, three in the very beginning. I kept a few training clients and pushed my sessions to as late in the day as possible. This way I had time to write jokes and be awake enough to go bomb at the clubs.

With time and commitment, I gained competency and built up to twenty-minute sets that I would perform nightly, often at more than one club. I was able to work at Caroline's and The Comedy Cellar alongside some of my idols. It is a high like no other; when the crowd is with you, it's like mainlining validation serum into your soul. I would leave the stage buzzing, vibrating with good feelings, and then I'd head back home at around three in the morning. Once home, I could not fall asleep.

I tried watching television, but the moment I get wrapped up in a program or a movie, I can forget about sleeping. Then I discovered infomercials can be a great snooze aid. I know far more about useless products that sell for $19.95 (if I call right now) than anyone should know. This worked for a couple of weeks, until I bumped into a segment of paid programming on animal rescue. There were all breeds of dogs in varying states of decay—mangy, shaking, sickly, malnourished, and begging for some unconditional love. Try as I might, I could not turn away. Watching animals that had been so horribly abused and then abandoned made me cry like a baby. Though it was gut-wrenching, I kept watching.

I didn't realize it at first, but this was what I'd been looking for, and I'm not talking about crying myself to sleep. I really enjoyed helping people as a personal trainer, but dogs had a much stronger pull on my heart. They don't have a voice, they can't help themselves, and, God knows, they don't hurt a soul. Like Mark Twain said, "If you pick up a starving dog and make him prosperous he will not bite you. This is the principal difference between a dog and a man." Dogs are good down to the marrow and loyal to a fault, and the images of those rescues haunted me day and night. It was a couple of weeks later when fate intervened and I met Robyn in Union Square.

The first dog Robyn asked me to foster was a young pit bull named Champ. He was white, with a beige patch around his left eye, a red nose, and about seventy pounds of taut, vibrating muscle. Robyn thought we'd be a good match, and I was so excited that I spent some of my limited resources on a giant crate, toys, dog food, treats, and an assortment of bowls.

When Champ and I first got to my apartment, things were fun. I served him some treats, and he followed me around as I gave him a little tour of my place. After that, I petted him some and sat down. Champ kept looking at me, and I thought, "Now what?" I had no idea. My mom's shih tzu didn't take up so much space and occupied himself if you left him alone. Didn't Champ have some business to attend to? I sat on my couch, and Champ sat a few feet away, just looking at me. It made me a little nervous. This went on for about twenty minutes, and I realized how different it was to be alone with a pit bull in a confined space versus being surrounded by experienced volunteers in an open, public place. Suddenly, he started barking, and I got more nervous. I had no idea what he was trying to communicate. Was he freaked out? Was he angry at me? Was he going to have a flashback and attack? He grabbed a rope toy and started growling and whipping it around in his mouth. I was beginning to really worry as he violently swung the rope toy. Was this a display of aggression? I wanted to put him in his crate and regroup, but I was scared to approach. I went into my bedroom and quickly shut the door behind me. Champ waited on the other side, barking. Eventually, he quieted down and I ventured out into my living room to find Champ very civilly sitting on my couch, chewing the rope toy. He appeared in good spirits and came toward me with the rope in his mouth. I mumbled, "Hey, buddy," and he started growling and shaking the toy again as if he wanted it dead. Scared, I bolted into the kitchen, grabbed some treats, and threw them into his crate. Champ dropped the rope toy, ran into the crate, and I shut the door behind him and exhaled. What was wrong with this dog and how did people deal with it? I didn't have time to contemplate the answer, because the moment he finished eating he started barking again. Deep, powerful barks. I figured he wanted out of the crate, and while I liked that idea in theory, in reality, he was staying put. I called Robyn, who cheerfully suggested he needed a walk. She was so matter-of-fact about it. I said, "Maybe he wants to kill me and then go for a walk," and she just laughed. I didn't have the courage to tell her that I was sincerely afraid. She did suggest that I wait until he calmed down before taking him out, and I enthusiastically agreed. I hung up to see Champ clawing at the door of his crate and scratching up the thick plastic floor. He continued to bark for almost an hour, or an eternity, if you have neighbors. After the barking marathon, he started whimpering and my fear turned to sympathy. I wanted to take him out and saw an opportunity when he fell asleep. I grabbed his leash and tiptoed toward the crate when Champ heard me. He popped out of his slumber with a vengeance and commenced with that throaty bark again. I thought, "If he doesn't kill me, my neighbors are going to." I took a deep breath, opened the crate, and quickly hooked the leash to his collar. Off we went, and Champ's strength was astounding. He pulled me down the block, sniffing and peeing on everything in sight. Maybe five minutes into the walk, Champ grabbed the leash in his mouth and started thrashing and growling. I vainly tried to wrest it from him and feebly said, "Champ, stop!" Guess who didn't listen? Good guess. I threw his leash around an iron fence post and stepped back. Within seconds, Champ dropped the leash from his mouth and commenced with that barking again. Defeated, I sat on a stoop and called Robyn. "I'm sorry, I think this guy is too much for me to handle."

"What's all that barking?" was her funny response. Thankfully, Robyn was in the area and offered to come by. I accepted her offer and thanked God.

I felt utterly helpless as Champ just barked and barked. Robyn showed up just in time to break my chops: "What's the matter, tough guy, this one got too much bark for ya?"

She took the leash, and Champ grabbed it and started thrashing once more. Robyn tugged back at it playfully and growled at Champ. The two of them played tug-of-war for a minute. Robyn stopped playing, and Champ let go of the leash about ten seconds later without making a sound. "Good boy," she said, and petted him. I felt like a total failure.

In order for Champ to return to the shelter, another dog needed to leave. This meant I would get my shot at redemption that very night. Up next was a jet-black Lab/pit bull mix named Momma. I knew her from the park, where she was an easy, super-friendly dog. She wasn't as boisterous as Champ but had some confidence issues that I learned about in a hurry. She was not easy to approach. Moving too quickly or reaching over her head to pet her caused her to duck down and growl in displeasure. I tried to entice her with the rope toy, to no avail. Frustrated, I whipped a toy across the room, and when it squeaked, Momma was all over it. It was a panacea: Whenever she seemed nervous or down, I would grab the squeaky toy to get her back in good spirits. We became fast friends thanks to that squeaky toy and she was a dream dog, save for her issues around food.

Around her food bowl, Momma would hover but not eat. When I got too close she would give me a sideways look or lower her head and let out a wicked growl. She never did this when I fed her treats or peanut butter from a spoon. Clearly, she was territorial around her food bowl and I was stumped.

At the time, I knew one trainer; a Russian guy named Igor who had trained police dogs in the former Soviet Union, which is nothing short of badass. I called him and, sure enough, he gave me some great tips. Since I was able to feed Momma treats without a problem, Igor suggested that I sit sideways, alongside her empty bowl, and place one piece of turkey in it at a time. He didn't want me facing the bowl because she may have felt threatened. When Momma would finish one piece of turkey, there would only be an empty bowl to guard. I immediately tried this out and right away she looked to me for the next piece of turkey. (It was so satisfying to see this work that I fed her about a pound of turkey.) The next day I would place two pieces in the bowl, and she tolerated my presence just as well. By the end of the week, I was able to put down a full bowl of dry food and turkey and sit right next to her. It had become a nonissue. Food aggression is the kind of difficulty that gets dogs sent back to the shelter, so I felt great about being able to help her. About a month later Momma got adopted, and it was an extremely happy moment in my life.

I continued to foster dogs and learned a little more from each one. Feeling competent I decided to head to the Bronx to see Robyn and meet all her foster dogs. Before I even got to her gate, I saw at least three pit bulls roaming the roof and barking to signal my arrival. Somewhat nervously I entered into a very modest two-bedroom home that had become a makeshift shelter. In Robyn's words, her home had "gone to the dogs." When I was there, there were no fewer than ten dogs and an equal number of cats. Robyn's heart was clearly bigger than her home.

Princess, the spunky pit bull/border collie mix, had been tossed over the fence into Robyn's yard a few weeks earlier. She had become a house favorite with her dark brindle/white coat and adorable spotted ears. Although only five months old, Princess spent her time running from room to room, nipping at the heels of the other dogs in an effort to herd them. She was often successful in corralling dogs three times her size before she'd abandon the project to jump in your lap and lick your face. It was as if she were saying, "See what I did?" because she would then run off and do it again. I was in love and told Robyn, "That's my dog."

I took her home and renamed her Chiquita. If there is a single dog that is responsible for my becoming a trainer, it's Chiquita. In the early going, the qualities that made her so fun were overshadowed by related qualities that made her difficult. Chiquita's rough start in life had turned her confidence into pushiness, exacerbated by a big dose of neediness. Her neediness caused her loyalty to turn into an aggressive form of protectiveness. Her great alertness often translated into feeling threatened and subsequently aggressive. Even on leash with me, she displayed aggressiveness towards people, particularly men. I knew it was fear-driven, so I was perfectly at ease with her, but my family was concerned for me. The day they came to meet her, she happily took toys and treats from them but also snapped at their fingers when they pulled away. When they got near her, she showed her teeth before running and hiding.

Once she got through a first meeting with someone, she'd generally be good, but unpredictability would reign for a while. I wanted my dog to live as stress-free as possible and became determined to see this through.

Some of the people I met through Robyn's rescue really *knew* dogs, and I spent more and more time with them. Igor was also very generous with his knowledge, and I greatly valued our daily phone calls. As I soaked up information from myriad sources I found conflict not consensus among experts. This was disheartening, until I realized that no one could know my own dog better than I. I would have to figure out for myself what was going to work for her. Chiquita was both sensitive and pushy. Training her like a gun-shy, sensitive dog was not going to work, nor would treating her like a strong-willed, pushy dog. I had to find a way to be nurturing while firmly setting limits. It was a finesse game and as I gained confidence in my abilities, her trust in me grew as well. The first thing to show improvement was her fear aggression.

I continually introduced her to new people, and was careful not to admonish her when she acted out. By not getting emotionally invested in her behaviors, I began to see her reactions as if they were happening in slow motion. She would back up in fear but being on leash forced her to hold her ground. The next move would be to lunge forward and snap but not bite. A confident dog wants to bite and hold, but a fearful dog will snap and pull back. Unfortunately, her lunging was in response to a friendly person stepping forward to say hello. To deal with this, I would have people stay where they were, and with a clear "ehh-ehh," I interrupted Chiquita's normal path to aggression. My poor baby was just scared, and I couldn't have this anymore than I could tolerate her snapping at people. As time passed, I could see the earliest signs of her discomfort, and I would interrupt her pattern. When strangers were a hundred feet away, I would get her attention on me. The moment she started fixating or "pinning" on a pedestrian I would disrupt the process. Pinning is when a dog's eyes lock on something with laser focus and I was now able to identify the earliest signs. It was essential that I was not the least bit fazed by her behavior. This made Chiquita, and the strangers I introduced her to, far more comfortable. Eventually, instead of reacting, she would look to me for instruction and I knew we were on our way.

I began to work at a dog care and training center a few blocks from my apartment because it had an indoor dog swimming pool. I love to swim, and so do most dogs. I brought Chiquita to work with me and learned from the instructors the finer points of "swimming" dogs. Swimming with Chiquita seemed to remove any lingering insecurity and, within a few weeks, I enrolled her in obedience classes that the school offered. I'm proud to say she took to them like a dog to water.

When Chiquita was eleven months, my girlfriend, Erin, and I went to an adoption event Robyn was throwing in Central Park.

Chiquita was having a great time playing with the other dogs, but she was especially drawn to a young male pit bull. The two of them got along swimmingly and this male pit may have been the most laid-back dog I'd ever met. If he could speak, I'd imagine he'd say "Sounds good" to most anything. Regrettably, he was covered in sores and suffered from a bad case of mange. Erin and I looked at each other and knew he needed to come with us.

I was now the beaming Dog Dad of a nine-month-old brindle pit bull I named Pacino. It took a good three months for him to return to full health, and once he was healthy, I began working commands with him and taking him to the pool.

I would swim Chiquita and Pacino before taking them and a couple of their friends from day care out by the Chelsea Piers to train. There was Buster, an aloof but lovable chow mix (proudly featured on the cover), as well as Sadie and Shadow, both black Labs that I had met in the pool. My dogs were in their adolescence and were very mischievous, but their temperaments evened out around their friends.

Chiquita and Pacino resembled teenage siblings who actually got along. They played hard together, challenged each other, and were best friends. Part of my style of parenting them was to let them work things out for themselves, which is important. When they both wanted the same toy, a little struggle would ensue, and I would not intervene. I find that dogs can solve most of their own problems without human intervention.

Outside of basic training and exercise, I would also exercise their minds. I'd have them play games that required problem solving, like placing a ball inside a box and letting them figure out how to open it.

If a toy ended up under the couch, I wouldn't automatically retrieve it for them and I learned that dogs are pretty adept at moving furniture when inspired. My aim was to have confident, self-assured dogs, despite the fact that they started out abused and abandoned.

They also gave me my share of trouble. I learned the hard way that my cable company has a limit on remote control replacements. For whatever reason, the dogs targeted the remote for the cable box and started pooping out buttons. They could also be tough on other dogs. Both Pacino and Chiquita are high-energy, driven dogs, so having a few older dogs to help socialize them was essential.

When I took them down to the Piers for training, Chiquita was quicker to learn than Pacino, but his mellow disposition made things go more smoothly. While one was training, the other would have to sit and stay. I believe that watching each other facilitated their learning and taught them patience.

When Pacino was learning to fetch, he couldn't understand that I wanted the ball brought all the way back to me. When he fell short of his target, Chiquita would fetch his ball, drop it at my feet, and then paw at my hand for his reward. Pacino, for his part, had difficulty waiting out any type of tug-of-war game. When it involves biting or being petted, he wants in at all costs. Impulse control could have been a big problem for two pit bulls in the big city, but these exercises in patience afforded them some much-needed self-control. The carryover was obvious, as things like jumping on company, begging for food, or even fighting over a ball became much less of an issue.

Dogs were my life now—I became a regular at the dog park— and spent hours with professional dog walkers, learning about their respective packs. Dog walking is a skill unto itself and something of an art form. It requires one to have enough vision to read the road ahead while being able to make fine adjustments on the leash. Caring for dogs in the park requires similar abilities. Skilled walkers can read the energy of the park the moment they step into it: A quick scan and they can tell you who and what to look out for. Certain dogs are going to cause trouble, and you can see it in the way they play. Knowing who and what to keep your dog away from is everything. It's an acquired skill that will come to most people who don't text or live on their cell phones at a dog run. But dog walkers know the park better than anyone, down to the specific dynamics between individual dogs and people.

I loved learning about dogs. I loved the work of it, and I loved the relaxation of it just as much. There was nothing better than coming home from performing comedy, lying on my couch, and just watching my dogs. It was my version of staring at a fireplace. For a high-strung person like myself, the passive observation of dogs at play was meditative and therapeutic.

At the day care center I began to watch volunteers, dog trainers, and employees teaching commands. I had definitely gotten the hang of it with my dogs and their buddies, but not every dog I worked with responded so well. I watched people try all types of approaches and among them was a group I dubbed the "supers": super-sweet, super-stern, super-loud, super-soft, super-happy, even super-neutral (think monotone). The supers were equally effective or ineffective, depending on your point of view. Some dogs seemed to get it, while others did not.

One woman, who was not a dog trainer, had far more luck working with dogs than most. I wondered what she might be doing differently and began to really watch her. I noticed she was far less vocal than most people and was much more rigid, though not stiff, in movement. She had excellent posture, which I soon learned meant something. Standing tall lends a certain authority, and a person with good posture has a great head start in teaching commands. I had noticed myself that bending down to repeat instructions never worked. When this woman spoke, it was in a happy but very even tone of voice. She made an effort to establish eye contact with the dogs. The eye contact got her the dog's attention and by being economical in speech and movement, the dog remained focused. A few days after seeing her work wonders, I ran into Igor and explained my findings. He was amused to hear that I'd observed something that was so ingrained in him. He confirmed my findings and showed me a whole host of hand signals he used in training. His movements were military in their precision and always minimal.

To outside observers the woman at the day care appeared to have a little magic up her sleeve. The dogs clearly followed her movements and learned commands quickly under her tutelage. She was even-tempered and patient, low-key but upbeat, precise in her movement, stood tall, and had an intuitive ability to make and maintain eye contact with a dog. These qualities would have made her an ideal trainer. In short order, I incorporated better posture and a more even demeanor into my training. I also began to wait for a dog's eyes to meet mine and the results were immediate.

At home, I educated myself as best I could and learned that dogs are incredibly adept at picking up cues from our eyes. Growing up I had been told that looking directly into a dog's eyes could invite aggression. Not so. It is just wise to avoid engaging in a pre-fight stare-down when meeting a new dog. Some of the reading I did on dogs and dog training was enlightening while much of it seemed suspect. I became more invested in my own experience and observation to guide me. What I did find interesting was that many animal trainers seemed to know more in the early twentieth century than we do now. Back in the day, it was more common to be an animal trainer, not specifically a dog trainer. These people worked with animals of vastly different sizes and constitutions. Many of the animals they worked with also posed high levels of danger. Punishment-based training is not a great option with a lion, so trainers needed to persuade the animal to follow their suggestions or face a serious occupational hazard. They were master problem solvers whose jobs got specialized as they split into factions of dog trainers, elephant trainers, and the like. I believe that when this happened, those without the great education of working with different types of animals began to take shortcuts, which gave rise to rudimentary and too often inhumane training. The good animal trainers had finely honed instincts and an understanding born out of experience, and I wanted the same for myself. I can't imagine a better apprenticeship than training animals in general, but, living in New York City, I would have to cut my teeth on dogs.

The one unimpeachable fact that I took away from my reading is that a dog trainer is a problem solver. My first conclusion as a problem solver was that every dog has a unique pathway to learning and inventiveness may be required. Some dogs respond well (and happily) to demanding personality types who try to exact perfection. Other dogs appear lost and even discouraged. It still shocks me that few concessions are made for the individual nature of each dog being trained.

At the day care, I began to notice a pattern. Every person had a particular way of working with dogs, and no matter how a dog reacted, no one really adjusted his or her approach. When frustration set in, they would then attempt the same thing twenty percent louder or quieter, twenty percent faster or slower, or some combination of both. Naturally, certain people claimed that some dogs were "better" than others. It would have been more accurate to think, "The one thing I do works better with some dogs than others." No one took a look at how the dog was reacting. The only thing noted was the success or failure of a command. There was also too much debate surrounding how to treat the dogs. Many owners wanted their hardened shelter dogs treated like they were made of glass. For example, two poorly trained German shepherds (that listened to no one) spent their days biting and snarling at each other in play, but their owners only wanted them to hear hushed tones and happy sounds. Dogs would keep each other in line by using their powerful jaws on thickly padded necks while workers debated over collars and leash pressure. Overbreeding causes certain dogs to have weaker tracheas than others, and this needs to be respected, but if a dispassionate, uncaring person wants to choke a dog with a leash, he certainly can, regardless of the collar. Why the need for such standardization? Wasn't it obvious that some dogs responded differently than others?

I spent all my spare time with Chiquita and Pacino. They would fight for toys and get riled up enough to scare visitors, but I now knew all their tells. When Chiquita would begin to turn her head away in apparent anger, things could escalate. On a one-to-ten scale, their intensity always had to stay below a seven. Chiquita can be short-tempered while Pacino has the alpha personality and, despite his laidback demeanor, is no pushover. A dog's energy levels ebb and flow in a manageable fashion until the threshold gets crossed. I call seven the tipping point. When a dog gets to that point, there is no quickly turning back. Altercations can take place, or a dog will be unreachable and require a significant wind-down period. The good news is that the alpha personalities, contrary to what people think, know who they are and don't need to assert themselves so readily. They are apt to let a toy go in a tug-of-war or even let a "lower-ranking" dog have the last bite of food. It's the insecure dogs, vying for "street cred," that cause all the ruckus.

Between my dogs, their friends, the fosters, and the day care, it was abundantly clear that dogs were now the central preoccupation in my life. As if this weren't enough, they introduced me to a subculture that was right under my nose. Although I've never been shy or short on friends, being able to stop and say hello to so many people is a nice incentive for having dogs. Thanks to my dogs, I look like the mayor of my block.

I am also not opposed to offering help, and this got me a little notoriety as one of the good dog people in my neighborhood. When I saw people struggling to work with their dogs on the street, I could often spot the breakdown in communication and fix little issues in no time. As time passed, people started asking me for help, and I always obliged. It was a time of great learning and practice. My neighbors began to claim that I had the animal equivalent of a green thumb.

After I helped Barbara, my neighbor and friend from the day care, teach her chow, Buster, the "down" command, she asked me an intriguing question: Would I like to watch Buster for a holiday weekend? I quickly answered yes. I was honored that someone who didn't know me all that well would trust me with her dog and when I went to pick up Buster, a funny thing happened—she paid me. It had never crossed my mind to accept payment for having a dog stay at my house. I had kept many rescues at my place without any thought of remuneration. It then occurred to me that I could make a living by working with dogs. I became a part-time walker for Buster. I taught him to sit while waiting for traffic lights, along with some general etiquette. Barb recommended me to her friend, and, in short order, a (really) small business formed. It was just in the nick of time. My personal training clients were dwindling, and I was not able to support myself solely from stand-up comedy. My days began to consist of walking dogs, training dogs, boarding dogs, spending time at the day care, and performing stand-up comedy. It was a great time in my life. Chiquita and Pacino became incredibly useful in helping to socialize and rehabilitate neighborhood dogs. They were my partners and perfect introduction partners, as well. It was common to see dogs with leash aggression or fear experiencing overall improvement when they learned a proper introduction. Being able to successfully meet another dog is the gateway into socialization, and no one teaches this better than my dogs. Their temperaments are perfect because they're polite but quick to put a dog in its place. They require some monitoring, but I make little adjustments on the fly and don't worry about belligerence. Dogs that got too up in their business quickly learned how to be more polite, while fearful dogs could sense Chiquita's and Pacino's self-possession and became more comfortable. After we would rehabilitate a new dog, that dog would join the "staff" to help me work with the next dog. Within a few months, I had a cache of about ten dogs that were well equipped to handle any dog-on-dog issues. Depending on the degree of difficulty, I could choose from the group, from easiest to hardest. My cavalier King Charles named Stella may be the most polite dog I've ever met, so fearful dogs would start with her and work their way up to the larger dogs.

Though my life was just about perfect, I had some unfinished business with shelter dogs. Every time I fostered a rescue and was fortunate enough to find a home for it, I gained new respect for the people who give their time to shelters and rescues. It is heartbreaking work, and I admit that I do not have the stomach to be in the trenches on a daily basis. Although I was extremely busy with my burgeoning dog care company and slowly gaining steam as a comedian, I was dying to help.

After performing a few sets of comedy around town, I took Pacino and Chiquita for a late-night walk and had an idea. I decided to combine my two passions—comedy and dogs—and my charity, Funny for Fido, was born. By leveraging my contacts in comedy, I was able to put on a charitable event at the legendary comedy club Caroline's, all in an effort to save homeless animals. The comedy community is tight-knit, and comedians are a very down-to-earth group of people, always willing to lend a hand. The charity immediately got traction when the dog owners I knew offered to pitch in. With a few calls, I had a great lineup of comedians slated to perform. Buster's mom, Barbara, is an event planner who really took the reins to make Funny for Fido a thriving charity. It was amazing to see this wave of support to help an organization that provides financial grants to animal rescues and shelters. Colin Quinn, Dave Attel, Jim Gaffigan, Amy

Schumer, and the late, truly great Patrice O'Neal have all performed at this annual event, now in its sixth year. We have raised money to pay for veterinary care, food, training, and transport as well as temporary and permanent housing for animals that are essentially on death row. It is perhaps the accomplishment I am proudest of.

I was also gaining more experience as a trainer. I secretly called myself a dog re-trainer, because nearly all the dogs I trained were obedience school dropouts that had also failed with other trainers. I found working with the dogs easy enough, but conveying the lesson to the client was challenging. The minute I left the session, I was rarely confident that the owners could implement the fix. Were the dogs I trained my own, there wouldn't have been any of these issues, so I had trouble relating to my clients' difficulties. This would be my Achilles' heel until I coaxed my best friend, Dave, into helping me. Dave had come back to New York a year or so earlier and moved back into his apartment. As fate would have it, my new place was just a few blocks away.

Dave is the big brother I never had. I often say that he is to people what I am to dogs. He is one of the most observant, astute people one will ever encounter. I knew he would be a natural with the dogs, but I *really* needed him to act as a liaison between the clients and me. Figuring out what's wrong with a dog is quick, but if I can't get the client to realize what I'm saying or how he might be contributing to the problem, the dog will continue to suffer. I credit Dave with helping me understand that we truly train people as much as or more than dogs. He continually challenges me to put myself in the client's shoes and is great at getting people to open up about their personal difficulties. He appeals to people's love for their dogs, and pretty quickly, sticking points are overcome. He knows a fair amount about quite a few things, and when I first mentioned the warring schools of thought on positive versus negative reinforcement, he shrugged, and said, "B. F. Skinner," before quoting him: "The consequences of behavior determine the probability that the behavior will occur again." He explained a little about how rewards and punishment determine our courses of action. It was eye-opening for me to learn that most of the people engaged in the debate on positive versus negative reinforcement were both uninformed and misinformed. Although the material isn't particularly exciting, Dave made sure I understood it. Skinner has definitely influenced me and lent some clarity to my dog training. In fact, B. F. Skinner's work is responsible for what is probably the most boring part of this book (the second half of Chapter 4, in case you want to jump ahead), and we all have Dave to thank for that. All kidding aside, I often say that if I'm the go-to guy for dogs, then he's the go-to guy for the go-to guy for dogs.

With this newfound knowledge I realized that the world of dog training is largely made up of opposing fragments, with each individual sect trying to gain notoriety as "the way." It seems everyone has one particular approach that's bulletproof. I truly believe that many training programs are simply too trainer-centric and don't focus enough on the dog, let alone the dog's owner. What I mean by "trainer centric" is that trainers often have a set way of doing things and apply their singular methodology regardless of how the dog reacts. Trainers need to adjust and adapt to the dog and client that is being trained, not the other way around. My ongoing experience as a re-trainer continues to prove this point. A dog will attempt to communicate via body language, energy level, and drive. The clues are easy to miss if you're not looking for them. "Drive" is a term used to describe a dog's intrinsic level of motivation to perform a behavior. Prey drive and food drive are the most commonly referenced, but when I look at a dog, I ask myself, "What's *driving* the drive?"

In the case of Harry the bulldog, fear was creating a strong drive to not walk. He became the poster child for what Dave was saying about owners creating or contributing to a dog's difficulties. Handsome Harry was a stubborn bulldog that would not walk on leash. He was not a "halter," in the classic sense—a dog that walks and periodically stops without warning. Harry would consistently stop walking and appear near catatonic when he got roughly a hundred feet away from his building. No matter which direction he went, this would happen. When a dog checks out like this, the most effective technique is to keep his chin up to prevent him from going into shutdown mode. The "keep your chin up" approach did not work with Harry, which surprised me.

Every dog spends a fair amount of time looking at the ground and sniffing, and Harry was no different. His eyes and nose were doing the right thing when he walked, until his head would bow and presto—you had a bulldog with four flat tires. Even food would not budge him, and Harry had a strong food drive. The fact that he wasn't taking the bait suggested that stress was shutting down his digestive system. I needed to get to him before that shutdown occurred.

I took a close look at the way Harry walked. When we kept his chin up and he didn't have the option of dropping his head, he would close his eyes and halt a few seconds later. When we didn't keep his chin up, a magnetic pull seemed to cause Harry's head to drop about six inches, and he'd go kerplunk. The trick was not to stop his head from dropping but to keep his eyes open.

In this case, a surprisingly simple, consistent cue in the form of a leash tug and a happy "Hey, Harry!" kept his attention and got him past the danger zone. Harry's neck rivaled Mike Tyson's in girth, so I wasn't worried about a bit of leash pressure. After this, he was good for the rest of the walk. It had been the bane of his owner's existence and that of every trainer and walker who came before me. It may have looked like magic, but all it took was some careful observation.

Before I worked with Harry, I took the time to get his history to see if there were any inciting events that may have caused him to turtle up. There were no identifiable causes; Harry had a clean bill of health from the vet and no traumas to speak of. His owner was a nervous guy who did not look well suited for the rough neighborhood where he resided. Dave's theory was that the owner would take him for his late-night walks and become fearful when he got more than a short distance from home. This caused Harry to inherit the fear response and freeze. I believed Dave was right, but we both agreed that fixing the stubborn bulldog was a better option than trying to cure this poor guy's fears. The owner was extremely grateful but strangely unwilling to implement the fix on a regular basis. Invariably, I would get a call from him telling me Harry "did it again." When I asked him if he was doing what I suggested, he basically complained that Harry shouldn't be that way in the first place. It can be a tough gig sometimes.

It was a real shame, because Harry was a friendly, social dog that reveled in the company of people. Had he been skittish about making his way onto the bustling New York City streets, I don't think my technique would have worked.

At this point in my career, my training morphed into an approach that put equal emphasis on the owners. With a thorough pre-screening followed by a session, I could find a fix, but it would be up to the owner to implement it. My "after-sales" service would be encouragement and fine-tuning, not additional sessions. The owner needed to be empowered because the dog's responses were almost always predictable.

After the travails of Harry the bulldog, Dave insisted I do an owner "intake and assessment" before booking an appointment. Harry's owner had a tone in his voice that was uptight and closed off. In conversation, he spoke quickly and did not want to hear anything about Harry's difficulty. He made it sound like Harry was a computer that needed to be reprogrammed and that should be that. His attitude clearly suggested he might be the problem, but I didn't ask enough questions before we met. Nowadays, my pre-training conversations typically last about thirty minutes. There are a few main types of owners:

1. The ultra-loving dog owner who has overanalyzed the dog's behavior but never his own.

2. The person who has entirely unrealistic expectations and is perplexed—"Why does my dog sometimes, but not all the time and not always for long, bark at night?"

3. "Dog takeover"—a person whose life is run by his dog.

4. The person who is doing his best and needs a little help.

I began to train dogs from the suburbs to downright rural areas, including a dog that couldn't get along with the horses on a ranch. The rural dogs and client difficulties weren't that different from the city: There's an initial miscommunication that grows as parties drift apart and negotiations break down.

One day I got a call from a client who had recommended me to a woman developing an idea for a show about dog walkers. I almost didn't go, out of arrogance, as I now considered myself a trainer, not a walker. Dave set me straight, saying, "You're a dog guy, period," and he was right. When we first started working together, Dave insisted on walking dogs and I admired him for it. He had previously been the consummate self-employed professional, writing investment memorandum in highly technical trades. Although he would go on to streamline the business, he continued to walk dogs tirelessly and became an excellent handler himself. Despite Dave's pep talk, I was still tepid about this meeting but went anyway. When I showed up with Pacino, my attitude was not the best, and to make matters worse, the woman asked, "Is he gonna bite me?" It's kind of a pet peeve of mine that people feel such stigma toward pit bulls, so I dropped the leash and Pacino ran up to her and licked her face. She was instantly charmed, and when I showed her how Pacino jumps into my arms so we're chest to chest, she was sold. This woman really drank the Pacino Kool-Aid, because the next step was meeting with a roomful of producers from CBS. The story producers were all dog lovers and owners, and an instant connection was made. Our pitch meeting turned into a dog question-and-answer session, and from idea to airing, the show—*Dogs in the City*— was put together in near record time. It was the result of being the right person in the right place at the right time. The experience was incredible, and I appreciated the care the network took in presenting a show that depicted the reality of what I do.

After the show aired, Dave and I were inundated with training requests. Our training radius expanded greatly but the issues remained the same. For owners, it is paramount to know your dog and to keep an open mind that sees past his limitations and focuses on his wondrous capabilities. When people do this they often discover their own snags and overcome them. While dogs can all benefit from a trainer's instruction they do best when learning from an owner who attempts to understand them.

I also think we need to adjust our expectations and understand that they are dogs; they are going to engage in canine behaviors.

Since the show, I've had the fortune of training hundreds of dogs in a pretty short period of time and still log countless hours boarding them. They have provided me with a learning experience that has done far more for me than I could ever do for this great species. It is my hope to share this experience so you may partake in the loyalty, love, and compassion that dogs have so freely given me.

A NOTE ON READING

As my editor so succinctly said, "People will buy this book because their dog is peeing on the couch." While that certainly makes sense, I try to avoid focusing on the immediate fix. It's more important to address a dog's behavior and the owner's response to that behavior. It is a rare dog that has only one behavioral tic. It is my aim to teach dog owners "how to fish so they eat for a lifetime." Once that base of knowledge is laid, much of what I do is predicated on touch, feel, and sense. I had to consider how to best communicate this via the written word.

Prescriptive nonfiction books written on dogs typically fall into two categories: 1) philosophical in nature and somewhat inaccessible; and 2) highly instructive and hands-on. Instruction manuals don't work well because they do not consider the dog being taught or the person teaching the dog, while the more philosophical books usually contain better information but it can be very difficult to apply. For this reason, I wanted to try and do both.

I believe the very best thing a dog owner can do is look at their dog with new eyes. When we consider what incredible animals we have the fortune of being paired with, it is not unreasonable to think that we, not they, have to adjust our mind-set. The instructive chapters are important for practical advice, but if you go straight to them, the real learning will be missed.

It is essential to understand the basics of training, but it is more important to connect to your dog. To do so, you must listen with your eyes and be less reactive. When you slow down and see what's going on, the fix may be right in front of you. "Why is my dog pulling me on the leash?" is a question I've been asked a thousand times. How do dog owners typically react to a pulling dog? They give in and let the dog walk them or they pull back so both parties are doing the same thing—pulling. Although the owner may win this tug-of-war, the dog thinks it's a game or a test of wills so chalk up a small victory for the pooch. When the dog pulls and the owner follows, the practice of pulling is effective for the dog and he earns yet another victory. At this point, owner frustration sets in and in an effort to reach a state of détente, the dog owner negotiates and buys a collar or harness that makes pulling less painful for the dog. This is far different from getting a collar that helps train the dog not to pull. A less reactive and more observant walker may stop and not move. What happens then? Even the most stubborn dog will eventually stop pulling, look back, and say with his eyes, "What do you want me to do?" This is the window of learning for the dog and owner.

To open that window and keep it open requires more than a fix of the individual issue; it requires an overhaul of perspective. This book is written with that perspective in mind. The list of commands and the answers to common problems are actually the smaller pieces to the puzzle.

Finally, regarding gender, I use both "he" and "she" on occasion, as well as the neuter pronoun of "it" when not referring to a specific dog. I realize that dogs are never an "it," but I opted to do this for the sake of simplicity. I truly do not wish to offend anyone. I also don't consider myself an "owner" of a dog—my dogs own themselves—but again, for the sake of simplicity, I refer to dog moms and dads as owners.

CHAPTER 2

WE'RE ONLY HUMAN

"Dogs are, after all, man's best friend.
The least we can do is try to understand them a little better."
—NICHOLAS DODMAN

Every dog inherits a set of personality traits from its parents. Genetics determine things like herding instincts, energy levels, drive, and function. A lapdog's function is to sit idly in its owner's lap and look pretty. Naturally, its energy and aggression levels are pretty low, and it will never attempt to rustle up cattle or herd sheep. Retrievers used for waterfowl hunting must exhibit a Zen-like calmness because the hunting is done in small boats in winter conditions. Many hunting breeds, such as retrievers, poodles, and cocker spaniels have what's known as a "soft mouth," referring to their ability to pick up, hold, and gently carry quarry. It is almost impossible to teach this behavior to a dog without the inborn ability, and although I'm not a proponent of hunting, it is an impressive skill set. Terriers, on the other hand, are expected to shake rodents and snakes in order to kill them quickly and efficiently, so a soft mouth in this breed would be a very rare exception and a problematic one.

Breeding has gone a long way to make certain characteristics predictable. Once we set aside these characteristics, each dog still has a unique personality paw print. Distinct from the business of nature and nurture, dogs have leanings, preferences, and moods that are expressed in an entirely individual manner. It is imperative that we know some of our dog's special ways and put them to good use. Were dogs fluent in English, the first thing they would do is assure us that they're positive what they're doing is okay. In fact, they could cite chapter and verse on how their behaviors are approved by their owners.

We domesticated dogs, and nowadays, their value lies primarily in companionship. They are no longer on the periphery of our villages, waiting to feast upon scraps. We've pulled them closer and closer and expect them to socialize and integrate flawlessly in our changing world. They've done a pretty remarkable job, and yet we stretch them to the point where anthropomorphizing is actually trendy. They wear raincoats as if nature forgot to consider rainfall in their evolution; they sit in handbags wearing sweaters at cafés; they accompany us to work on occasion and are expected to be polite to our guests at home. The reality is that dogs are not plug-and-play little people with four legs. They're dogs, which means they have minds that don't work like ours.

> *Were dogs fluent in English, the first thing they would do is assure us that they're positive what they're doing is okay. In fact, they could cite chapter and verse on how their behaviors are approved by their owners.*

BY ANY OTHER NAME, IT'S A DOG

Babies cry and dogs bark. And chew. And eat things that make us yak. They chase, sniff, bite, dig, pull, lunge, bury bones, hide food, and pee on things the way graffiti artists "tag" walls with spray paint. The good news is that dogs are far more reasonable, team-spirited, and adaptable than humans. Dogs come equipped with a set of sensory skills that would make the X-Men jealous, a neural net formidable enough to know my landlord is coming to collect the rent long before he knocks on my door and an incomparable facility to take cues from us with their eyes. A study published in the February 2004 *Journal of Comparative Psychology* found that dogs are much better than apes at understanding humans' cues to find hidden food. They are remarkable animals, but they're not perfect. Breeding and experience can render some dogs more aggressive, irritable, fearful, and antisocial than intended. Still, if a dog is reasonably well trained and properly socialized, it is always capable of fitting in.

Training allows us to connect to our dogs and give them a sense of purpose. Along the way, we can get these loyalists to do just about anything we want, as quickly as they can hijack an owner's life with their hijinks.

Training allows us to connect to our dogs and give them a sense of purpose. Along the way, we can get these loyalists to do just about anything we want, as quickly as they can hijack an owner's life with their hijinks.

3 6646 00233 3076

SPEAKING DOG

We've all seen someone who is "good with dogs." Everything looks easy and goes smoothly. So what's that all about? It's the power of observation. Dealing with dogs may *seem* intuitive for some people simply because they've learned to keep a keen eye on the animal. Most people are too inundated with their own concerns to do this, and we've got the troubled kids of the two- and four-legged variety to prove it.

A woman whose dog I trained was overfeeding and underexercising her schnauzer. She told me she did so because she wanted the dog to like her. She had concluded that her dog was ornery and malcontent because it didn't want to go outside and needed to be fed more. Oy vey. I immediately knew who didn't like going outside. After some reflection, she came to the realization that the dog's despondence, short temper, and bratty behavior began around the same time she started curtailing his time outside. After she admitted she had been spending too much time at work, we agreed to find her a dog walker. With some gentle nudging, she also became more proactive in taking her dog out. A month later she conceded that not only was her schnauzer in better spirits, her mood and general outlook improved. What did it? The simple act of taking her dog out for walks. Too many dog owners are missing out on a great thing.

UNDER THE HOOD

Some people insist their dog never listens; I can assure you that dogs pick up on everything. Even dogs that appear to have ADD can readily respond to commands. Similarly, the best-behaved dog can look right through you and not budge when implored to come. Dogs recognize the half-heartedness of a limp "Rover, stay" and will respond in kind by not listening. While they know exactly when we mean business and when we're preoccupied, it's a rare owner who can read his dog the same way.

Dogs have adapted so well to domestication that I can't blame people for humanizing them. That said, a walk around the block for a dog is anything but a Sunday stroll. A dog can detect contraband in a backpack a block away, know what your buddy ate for lunch, pinpoint a rat's location in a nearby sewer using ultrasonic hearing, spot a mosquito's movement as it beelines into a pile of leaves across the street, and then tell you what time those leaves fell. For an encore, it can do this in near darkness while making you feel like you're the only thing on the earth that matters. It's got more sensory input being thrown at it than we can imagine and a processor that puts the latest Intel chips to shame. A dog's senses hit the ground running at full speed even when pulled out of a dead sleep. Dogs are master observers and will pick up on nearly imperceptible shifts in our mood before they even happen. They know far more than we realize.

THE DOG PROBLEM

Despite the robustness of a dog's wiring, owners and trainers tend to profile a dog's problem as a hiccup caused by inherent limitations. They do not consider the dog itself—how it picked up the problem, where it may have gotten the wrong message, etc. When a problematic habit or behavior is spotted, the fix is too often a mechanical off-the-shelf solution. Considerations for a dog's personality and motivations are discarded. Indeed, when an off-the-shelf solution is effective, it is usually nothing more than an effort to either bribe or intimidate the dog out of doing something it thought was okay. In both of these scenarios, the dog's personality is being shaped in a less than desirable direction, because the symptom is not the problem. In due course, your best friend will find an equivalent behavior that will ultimately lead you to a new trainer, book, or technique.

POWER OF THE PERSONALITY

What exactly do I mean when I say "profiling the problem but not the dog"? I once worked with a dog named Maya—she was a feisty Lab with a mischievous soul and a strong body and spirit. I was the third trainer to come along. Maya obviously had been to school; she understood her commands, and yet no one was able to get her to follow instructions with any real consistency. By the time I got there, Maya was still stuck on "stay."

Her owner, Rachel, had been on the wrong side of dog ownership for months. Maya was entering adolescence as part Velcro Dog (sticking to Rachel, mainly) and part China Shop Bull. The moment Rachel stopped moving, Maya would be right on her. To make sure I understood, Rachel put Maya on her dog bed, told her to stay, walked away, and sat on the floor. Before Rachel had the chance to settle in, Maya was all over her. Maya appeared to be trying to meld eyeballs with her in an effort to conjoin their heads permanently. It was funny, but not for Rachel.

Two other trainers had taken two entirely different approaches. The first went straight into performing drills and proofing what he taught her. Proofing is a method of testing and improving a dog's handle on a command by changing variables—distance, environment, instructor, anything that makes a prompt or command different—and usually more challenging. Maya's ability to learn once you had her cooperation was not in question, but getting her to understand that commands are not optional requests was another story. Maya got a good report card, but when I spoke to the trainer, he was a little more honest: "Yeah, she's good. Sort of. Good luck getting her to stay on the bed. Great dog, though." I wasn't surprised to hear this. Rachel had noticed that Maya would grudgingly follow along as the trainer worked overtime, drilling her with commands. Rachel could also tell that Maya had no real desire to engage and appeared restless.

At first glance, Maya appeared to be an "in one ear, out the other" type of learner. The reason the first trainer's persistent approach didn't work was subtle but simple: Maya was mischievous and playful, even sneaky. She could learn from anyone if her innate traits and strengths were played to. It was clear that she only wanted to play and was going to check out if she wasn't interested. I realized I needed to make training a game, but a game with lots of structure.

Her first trainer was a good guy, but too much of a disciplinarian for Maya. He had unwittingly attempted to train the personality out of her via constant repetition. Suppressing Maya's playful side was counterproductive to her learning process. The trainer ended up in an ineffective power struggle with the dog.

Maya's second trainer also didn't quite pick up on her personal cadences. He didn't realize that if you gave Maya a finger, she'd take an arm. On this go-round, the trainer attempted to let Maya play herself out by taking her to the dog run for some ninety minutes. That was not going to happen because this dog could stay wound-up forever if left unchecked. He compounded this mistake by trying to teach her right outside the park. A dog park is a tough environment to compete with. It's like trying to teach a kid to read while his buddies are playing ball in plain view. Also not happening. Maya did not transition properly from play to learning to resting mode. She's rambunctious, so when her energy levels get high enough, she definitely needs a cool-down period and some structure in her environment.

Rachel needed to be able to sit and do some work, and Maya needed to stay by her bed. I had to teach Maya to associate going to her bed as a good thing in order to keep Rachel sane and allow Maya to wind down or else she would remain in a heightened state. We would make a game out of it.

I began in her trigger place: the dog bed in the living room. My first move was to be very up-tempo so Maya would get the impression that there was some fun to be had. I waved her over to her bed and exhorted her to come. When she would move away from the destination, I kept encouraging her to come back with an enthusiasm that bordered on maniacal. This is one area where being shameless pays off. I was all agog and waved Maya over like I was trying to get a kid to come see Santa Claus make his way down the chimney. Rachel looked alarmed for a moment and then began to laugh—until Maya started following instructions. Rachel's perplexed but entertained expression told me that she understood how a loony level of excitement can make a real difference. She was on board.

Here's how it worked:

■ I would lead Maya to her bed with enthusiasm, and she would come.

■ She would move off the bed, but the moment she did . . .

■ I would happily lead her back.

■ Repeat the above steps roughly five times.

■ When a curious Maya stayed put for a moment . . .

■ I introduced a treat, upping the ante.

■ When she decided to stay, she was rewarded with a treat.

■ She would wander off again: no reward.

■ I waited, caught my breath, and she came back.

■ I rewarded her again, and she stayed put.

■ I enthusiastically led her away from the bed.

■ She happily began to come back on her own.

I had given Maya a choice. I basically said, "You can go your own way and have no one to play with, or you can play this game with me and be rewarded for it." Instead of bribing her, I had given her a very easy decision to make. For Maya, enthusiasm was the key to convince her that she wasn't sitting in a classroom.

Once I'd captured her interest, it was easy to teach her to stay for longer periods of time. Treats were absolutely involved, but Maya was learning on her terms. I admit, there was more coaxing than commanding for a while. Being too cajoling is considered something of a no-no for dog trainers; there are those who think the lesson won't get imprinted with excessive enthusiasm or rewards. This is true for some dogs and not for others. What Maya needed to learn effectively was irrepressible enthusiasm. As Dave likes to quip, "Whatever it takes, no dog left behind."

Looking under the hood of this session, it was neither formal training nor a party—it was a puzzle for Maya to solve. She was led to a place where she was asked to stay. Although she didn't yet understand our motives, she was able to move and play with *purpose*. In short order, Maya figured it out. Her bed was no longer a prison. She was playing a game, and being on that bed was a part of it. By session's end, Rachel was able to sit on the floor, and Maya would come only when explicitly invited. For Maya, staying put gave her something to do; staying put became an actual activity that allowed her to calm down and often fall asleep.

The "structure" of having a place to go and something to "do" (remember, staying became a sort of activity for her) helped to manage Maya's energy levels. If you'd asked her what her job was, she would have said (quite quickly, I'd imagine), "Well, my job is to stay here, because that woman over there told me it's very important. I'm participating in my family life by doing this. I'm a very important part of this family, thanks for asking, now get out of my way, because I could be called to do something very important at any moment, thank you. Hey, how come I feel sleepy?"

Even healthy, high-energy dogs like Maya can see their good energy turn into anxiety when they're not provided with needed structure. Boredom is an enemy for both dogs and kids. Ask a bored kid what the problem is, and you will get the following answer: "I don't know what to do" or "I don't have anything to do." Dogs tell us the same thing with their actions.

Knowing to stay put when Rachel sat on the floor gave Maya something to do. Her energy was now channeled and her mind was at work. Until Maya was clear on her purpose and role within the family, her anxiety continued to spike, and she couldn't unwind. Most everyone thought she was just a hyper dog that would cause problems until the end of her days. Going forward, her energy levels began to rise and fall much more smoothly.

> *Boredom is an enemy for both dogs and kids. Ask a bored kid what the problem is, and you will get the following answer: "I don't know what to do" or "I don't have anything to do." Dogs tell us the same thing with their actions.*

It should now be apparent that working with a dog's specific personality can make all the difference. As we progress, it will become clear that speaking dog does not require anyone to be Dr. Dolittle. It simply begins with listening with our eyes and rethinking our approach.

ROLES AND RESPONSIBILITIES

Most people are asking two things of a dog trainer, although they're usually phrased in the form of a hundred questions and observations.

1. Why is my dog making me crazy?

2. Why can't I fix it?

Answer: People often underestimate their dog's capabilities and the importance of its role in the family.

Dogs (both domestic and feral) are classified as a subspecies of the gray wolf and are the first domesticated species. They have been best friends with humans for a long time and were believed to have shown up on the archaeological radar about ten thousand years ago. However, a University of California, Los Angeles, study found that dogs have been separate from wolves for the same amount of time that groups of wolves have been geographically separated. That is estimated to be a hundred thousand years, a full tenfold greater than previously thought. Interestingly, only one other mammal exhibits a similar genetic diversity and widespread mixed gene pool: humans.

WHO'S THE BOSS?

So who domesticated whom? For a long time, humans and their canine counterparts did not get along. In the sixth century B.C., Solon of Athens offered a bounty on every wolf killed. In the sixteenth century, under the rule of Henry VII, the last wolf in England was killed. The Scots considered their dense forests unmanageable for hunting down and killing all the wolves, so they burned down the forests. By 1930, there was not a single wolf left in the contiguous forty-eight United States. That's roughly fourteen hundred years of recorded contempt. Why? Wolves have been hunted for sport, for their hides, to protect livestock, and even to protect humans. In the last few hundred years, almost every culture has attempted to kill off wolves. They may be the most persecuted animal in history. Again, why? There is no clear answer, but the simple reason could be: Outside of humans, the gray wolf is the most widespread large land mammal on the planet and, historically, our biggest competitor for food. Despite being such a formidable threat, wolves were able to turn the tides. In a rare case of survival of the friendliest, less aggressive wolves used their powers of charm and persuasion to get a few scraps from villagers and, little by little, found their way deeper into our culture. Their evolution likely had an impact on ours.

Wolves and early dogs were outstanding hunters with healthy appetites: not exactly the kind of partners you look for in a shared hunt. It is highly likely that they approached us first and did so with shocking success.

Dr. Colin Groves, a reader in the Department of Archaeology and Anthropology in the Faculty of Arts at Australian National University, stated that early humans relied on dogs' ability to hear, smell, and see, and this may have allowed certain areas of the human brain to shrink in size relative to other areas (particularly smell and hearing). Dr. Groves added, "Dogs acted as humans' alarm systems, trackers and hunting aids, garbage disposal facilities, hot-water bottles, and children's guardians and playmates. Humans provided dogs with food and security. This symbiotic relationship was stable over

Dogs' benefit to society is myriad. Science is now finding quantifiable ways to express just why the rewards of dog ownership far outweigh the trouble.

a hundred thousand years and intensified into mutual domestication. . . . Humans domesticated dogs and dogs domesticated humans."

Dogs' benefit to society is myriad. Science is now finding quantifiable ways to express just why the rewards of dog ownership far outweigh the trouble. A Virginia Commonwealth University study showed that employees who took their dogs to work produced lower levels of the stress-causing hormone cortisol. Another study cited that in stressful job situations, people who had their dogs with them experienced an eleven percent drop in stress, while those who did not have dogs had a whopping seventy percent increase in stress. Employers who experiment with allowing dogs in the workplace should consider a "Don't Bring Your Dog to Work Day" and watch what ensues. Even therapists are getting on board, so it may be time to make some room on the couch. Deb Havill, a clinical social worker and therapist, conducts client sessions with her two rescue dogs. "Dogs were domesticated to be attentive to us," said Havill, who has two couches in her office: one for clients and one for the dogs (no need

In other words, if you're having trouble with your dog, maybe your stress levels are too high and you need to spend more time with your dog.

to make room). "It is natural for us to be around them, so to not be around them would be unnatural. We would be in an unnatural state."

In other words, if you're having trouble with your dog, maybe your stress levels are too high and you need to spend *more* time with your dog. Fascinating though it may be, you may be wondering what this has to do with dog training. The answer is everything. Dogs have played an evolutionary role in our lives for a long time. In order for them to fulfill this role, we have to redefine and consider what dogs need that they might not be getting.

GET A JOB

Although our earliest dogs may have charmed their way onto the periphery of villages, they didn't get to stay on good looks alone. As they evolved, they began to earn their keep and became hard-wired to perform tasks. Herding dogs can shepherd livestock for over eight hours a day without resting. Portuguese water dogs were bred to deliver messages from boats to shore and can swim and dive for roughly ten hours without a break. Basset hounds can trail scents from dawn to dusk, and their limits probably haven't been tested (the testers would get too tired to keep up). With domestication, dogs' appearance began to change as they became softer-looking (think spots and floppy ears), and continued breeding gave rise to specific physical characteristics and skill sets.

It is safe to say that most people can't give their dog the exercise it can handle, but many do not even provide the exercise they *need*. When an underexercised dog goes unattended, it will perform instinctual functions. Dogs may try digging holes in the living room, or hunting down a few rodents and offering them up to you as a gift, among other creative endeavors. A dog needs to be stimulated and integrated into the society that it resides in.

Many dog owners today can be compared to parents who give their kids everything *except* time and attention. To us, getting dogs to sit and stay is for their own safety and allows us to relax and not worry that our dogs are being unruly or meddlesome. To them, they are performing a function. As with Maya, doing nothing was doing something, and for her this made all the difference. She gained purpose and structure in her life and responded well to it. To teach a dog anything is to give it a function, purpose, and role in its life. Dogs do not have to fetch the paper to feel useful, but ideally they should have an idea what they are supposed to be doing in any given scenario.

NO FREE LUNCH

To help establish a role in the family for your dog, you must recognize that it has one in the first place. A dog's genetic profile predisposes it toward work, not companionship. In our culture, working dogs are in the minority. It is unlikely that your pet will be called upon to protect the family or flock, herd sheep, hunt down quarry, or perform a search and rescue. A dog's role is constantly in flux, especially as people's day-to-day routines become more demanding.

An emotionally healthy dog has a clear understanding of its role. This begins with the knowledge of who is capable of providing it with that role. In order to give a timid dog confidence, the dog needs to understand that it is not in charge of the household. The same holds true for an overbearing dog or a dog that exhibits "dominant" behavior. Whether a dog is overbearing, domineering, or even timid, such behavior reeks of anxiety and desperation for instruction. Why did I put "dominant" in quotes? Because there is a general consensus that since dogs are descendants of gray wolves, they are pack animals that adhere

> *Whether a dog is overbearing, domineering, or even timid, such behavior reeks of anxiety and desperation for instruction.*

to the protocols that govern a pack; ergo, one's dog will attempt to dominate and control its environment in order to establish its role as pack leader or be vanquished to mere subordinate. Sadly, many well-meaning owners are guilty of punishing their dogs in an effort to establish the role of alpha or pack leader. To put it mildly, that is a popular bit of hogwash.

John Bradshaw, the founder and director of anthrozoology at the University of Bristol, has studied the domestic dog for nearly thirty years. He states, "The most pervasive and pernicious idea informing modern dog training techniques is that the dog is driven to set up a dominance hierarchy wherever it finds itself."

It is not necessary for a dog's owner to establish him or herself as a leader, or "alpha" dog, because your dog has no desire to dominate you or run your life. In all likelihood, a household dog is not even a pack animal. Though dogs are lupine (related to wolves), it is absurd to assume that a dog will view a human as submissive or dominant and then attempt to establish its position in some mixed-species hierarchy. Research on Indian village dogs that live outdoors and survive on what they can find in garbage dumps fits the profile of non–pack animals to the letter. A village dog may bond with another but will remain mostly separate. These dogs do not hunt large prey in packs and are, by behavior, solitary scaven-gers who occasionally bond out of affection. If village dogs have lost their pack mentality, what can one expect from household dogs that have been domesticated for countless generations? As Bradshaw states, "Dogs do not set up wolf-type packs. They don't organize themselves in the way wolves do." His explanation for all the misin-terpretation? "People have been studying American timber wolves because the European wolf is virtually extinct. And the American timber wolf is not related at all closely to the ancestry of the domes-tic dog." Bradshaw contends that domestic dogs descended from sociable wolves, but "whatever the ancestor of the dog was like, we don't have it today."

Hopefully, we can move past our need to be withholding and militant in our approach to dogs so we can get back to the most enduring and successful business and pleasure rela-tionship in history. The most impor-tant thing for a dog to understand is that we *are* the rightful owner of those treats, chew sticks, and squeeze toys, and that we decide when the belly rubs get doled out. When your dog has learned this information, you will have a calmer and happier dog. Why? Because your dog has something to work for that will allow it to perform one of its biological imperatives. Think about it this way: If you get a check every month from an anonymous donor, you'll likely worry that one day the checks will stop coming. However, if you're confident that you have earned and will continue to earn

> *The most important thing for a dog to understand is that we are the rightful owner of those treats, chew sticks, and squeeze toys, and that we decide when the belly rubs get doled out.*

this check, you will not have cause for concern. It is healthy for a dog to know for whom and what they are working. Without this knowledge, the dog will feel unstable and be unable to bond. Dogs are fully dependent on us, and their desire to contribute to our well-being may be an encoded survival mechanism. Once it can say, "This is the person I'm working for, and this is what I have to do," it will no longer feel the anxiety of not knowing. Even if a dog is well provided for, not earning its keep will cause a dog to question the source of its bounty. To be perfectly clear: I am not suggesting that a dog will try to figure out what makes us happy. They are too smart for that, given that we humans are too fickle for them (in truth, they're not capable of that level of cognitive thinking). What makes us happy one moment may revolt us the next, so what do dogs respond to? Positive emotions. When we experience positive emotions, they will follow our lead. Remember how psychotically happy I pretended to be when I was urging Maya on? She wasn't following instructions at that point; she was following the good vibes. Dogs do have a biological urge to emotionally bond with humans, and this has intensified as we've continued to evolve toward each other.

This process is very different from establishing dominance, although an owner must be responsible for calling most of the shots. When I wait until my dogs are sitting calmly before I put the leashes on and take them for a walk, they are clearly aware that I'm setting the terms. It is up to me to initiate when work, play, exercise, and affection happen. This makes sense to them, because they understand what their role is in order to receive the things they desire. They know the rewards come from me, and I provide for them consistently, so they are well conditioned and thus relaxed. They also know what behaviors work in their favor, and these behaviors have slowly become their jobs.

LEADING THE HUNT

If you want a head start on creating a job for your dog, exercise is a great way to begin. Nearly all dogs are driven to be physical. However, giving a dog exercise does not mean opening the back door as you shout, "Fly, be free." As physical animals that need bonding, dogs need you to walk them, socialize with them at dog runs, take them swimming, or play fetch, among other possible activities.

Mental stimulation is equally important. I recommend that owners engage in an "active walk," wherein they teach their dog to heel as well as practice basic commands. Engaging the dog's mind while you're at play is a great stress reliever for both parties; it also gives your dog less time to consider getting wound up and misbehaving. For example, my dogs must earn their meals and playtime by training with me. By having them earn their keep, I convey to them that I hold the keys to the kingdom, which gives them that crucial purpose. To partake in my food, affection, and play, they will have to perform in order to secure it. This will prevent a world of unwanted behavior, so long as I don't expect perfection.

For example, Maya did not know what to do when Rachel sat down to do work. An owner's role is instrumental even in the passive part of a dog's life. We must observe what our dogs are doing in different environments so we may teach them appropriate rules of engagement. My dogs have free run of the house at times. They can run, wrestle, chew, and snarl at each other, and this works because they have other learned activities. If they did not know the "go to your bed" command, I'd be sitting there yelling, "Come on, that's enough now." From there I would have to separate them as a form of punishment, which is entirely unnecessary. I was once asked how my dogs separate play from chill time, especially in the same location. Great question.

Engaging the dog's mind while you're at play is a great stress reliever for both parties; it also gives your dog less time to consider getting wound up and misbehaving.

The answer is they may not consciously know how to transition from work to play, but there is a framework of commands that comprises the structure of a well-behaved dog. When I say, "Go to your bed," that effectively ends play for my dogs; if I say, "Drop it," then the toy in their mouth is no longer an option. Since dogs respond to positive emotions, I try to keep it light in tone and remember to offer treats on occasion for being cooperative. They may know these commands by heart, but the occasional treat can help them guard against selective forgetting. In the bigger picture, they also are rewarded by food, exercise, and affection.

To some degree, this may sound a bit dictatorial. I can see where some might be concerned, but it's possible to be a benevolent dictator who understands that a dog earning his keep will be a happy dog. When I did *Dogs in the City*, one of our most popular segments involved a skateboard-riding bulldog named Beefy. Beefy was a YouTube sensation and the head of the household. He would growl and groan whenever his owners got into bed together and would not relent until he was sleeping in between them. His owner Patrick is the nicest guy in the world, and his love for the dog allowed this behavior to continue. My purview allowed me to see that Beefy was a generally unhappy dog. He was demanding and whining, and when we were shooting, he appeared to have lost some of his verve about hopping on a skateboard. I told Patrick that I wanted to teach Beefy a new trick: how to be a dog.

Beefy was used to having his way, but more importantly, Patrick was used to giving it to him. Dave had a chance to talk with him on-set and discovered some interesting history. Patrick was newly married and had gone through a bad breakup a few years earlier. In the wake of the breakup, Patrick felt like it was him and Beefy against the world. Beefy could do no wrong where Patrick was concerned, and they spent an inordinate amount of time together. When Patrick met his wife-to-be, Erin, Beefy remained priority number one to Patrick, and the dog ran the house for a while. Erin was probably not particularly fond of this arrangement but didn't say anything. Beefy and Erin didn't have much of a relationship. In fact, Erin couldn't even walk him.

The first thing I did was convince Patrick that his seventy-pound bulldog would be happier with some limits and boundaries. It took some doing, but we agreed to a few ground rules. First, Beefy would have established feeding times and would no longer be allowed to sleep in bed with Patrick and his wife. Then we had Erin walk Beefy, because he had yet to warm up to her. We created a little space near the bedroom where Beefy could hang out and see in. Using a gate and leaving him in the kitchen would not have worked, because Beefy's protests would have kept everyone up all night. He also had to respond to Erin's commands before he would get fed. "Go to your bed," "sit," and "come" were practiced, and quickly, Beefy was listening to Erin. Once Beefy had to jump through a few hoops before he received the things he coveted, his disposition improved. Beefy had tasks to perform, and this sense of purpose put a little spring in his bulldog steps. Patrick had been trying to juggle his relationship with his wife and dog separately rather than integrating everyone into a little family.

This transformation illustrates my point perfectly. Having a job and "knowing its role" will fulfill a dog's biological needs. It is necessary for us to initiate, as well as stop, play, affection, and rewards. To be our very best at this, we must learn what motivates our dogs, to please them as well as to please us. When this happens, owners become more inclined to spend time with their dog and the horizon brightens. Play with purpose replaces head scratching and hair pulling. This begins with the passive act of watching our dogs.

CHAPTER 3

LISTENING WITH OUR EYES

"Saving just one dog won't change the world,
but it surely will change the world for that one dog."
—RICHARD C. CALL

Let's put ourselves in our dog's shoes for one moment. Assume you have had some repeated difficulties with your owners. After many attempts to understand the denizens of your domicile, you've made no progress. No matter what you do, your owners continually misread your every move. Your collar is heavy, and your paws feel tied.

The first thing that happens is someone in the house attempts to teach the sit command with a "No More Mr. Nice Guy" attitude. They act very stern and sound frustrated as they loudly say, "Siitttt, siitt." The dog is like: "I didn't understand what you wanted when you were being nice." Things remain unclear when a new person, aka "the good cop," intercedes and starts waving treats in a circle. Then the dog hears a long string of baby talk: "Wait, come, look at me, pay attention, good boy, good dog baby, now come, sit down, you

Whatever you've been taught about the right tone, stance, voice, and demeanor to use in dealing with dogs, forget about it. Had it worked, you wouldn't be reading this book.

can do it, that's it, come on come on puppy dog booby baby you can do it, sit, sit, sit down already, just sit, like this, sit, sit, sit." The dog thinks, "Huh? Come again?" It paces nervously: "That's a lot of words to learn . . . I don't know what any of them mean . . . how am I ever going to get that treat?" Every single word has a distinct meaning to a dog, even though it has yet to understand the monosyllabic "sit." The dog says to itself, "I'm gonna sit this one out." When there's more than one person in the household, the dog has probably never heard a unified, cohesive message. Typically, each person has tried a few approaches, tones, and timbres with little success.

There are a million wrong ways to do something and very few right ones. Whatever you've been taught about the right tone, stance, voice, and demeanor to use in dealing with dogs, forget about it. Had it worked, you wouldn't be reading this book. The only thing worse than the wrong message is a few of those wrong messages shaken, stirred, and watered down into a cocktail of misinformation.

PRESENT IMPERFECT

"Ever notice that perfectionists can never get it quite right?" So many dog owners try to be perfect, for all the right reasons, but they just end up missing out. I've trained innumerable dogs where the owner could tell me, down to the jots and tittles, what the dog is doing wrong, along with hundreds of reasons why they think their dog behaves poorly.

They never tell me what they think the dog is communicating or how, as owners, they might be executing poorly. In fact, I rarely hear anything about the dog doing something right. I've discovered time and time

> *It's essential to calmly detach and get a sense of what your dog is trying to communicate.*

again that the focus should always be on observing and not reporting. I cannot emphasize this enough. It's essential to calmly detach and get a sense of what your dog is trying to communicate.

THE ESPY

We're going to conduct a little experiment now, but first: There is only one solution to an underexercised dog—more exercise. It's irrational to give an animal built to work anything under an hour a day of brisk exercise. Now to our experiment.

Next time you come home, spend fifteen minutes not engaging your dog. Allow a momentary acknowledgment, then go about your business. Now keep an eye on your pooch. What happens within a minute? Usually, the dog will attempt to follow whatever your normal routine is with added vigor.

When this doesn't work, your dog will persist and possibly break into a whine. At some point, it will give up, but not without a fight. This is the common progression:

- The dog greets the owner with a "Come on down! You're the next contestant on *The Price Is Right!*" level of excitement (a client of mine named her dog Bob Barker).

- The owner matches the dog's level of excitement.

- The dog jumps, pees, nips, and freaks out in general.

- Vain efforts are made to chill the dog out.

- Owner invokes an abrupt "Okay, that's enough."

Bob Barker is a Yorkshire terrier that did not engage in the above sequence. He is also one of the first dogs I ever trained. When I first spoke to his whisper-quiet owner, Sheila, I was so thrilled to be training dogs that I didn't bother to ask about his issues. Between my excitement, Sheila's subdued voice, and Bob Barker's nonstop barking in the background, not much information was processed. I must have said "I'll be there" about ten times, hung up the phone, and actually made it to the subway station before I realized I didn't have the address. I made another call, got the address, and said "I'll be there" one more time. The only prep work I'd done was a little brushing up on the breed, which proved intimidating at the time: "Although classified as a toy breed, this is a terrier through and through," "can make a determined and boisterous watchdog," and finally, "even when properly trained, this dog will never be considered quiet." Uh-oh. On the subway I began worrying about how I was ever going to get this dog to stop barking. I arrived with no good plan.

Every trainer has a client in the early going who is notably unique or weird. Sheila is unique. She whispered on the phone like Marilyn Monroe, but when her door swung open, I was greeted by a woman who looked like a cross between the St. Pauli Girl and Zsa Zsa Gabor. She also spoke in a thick German accent at deafening volumes. Why would she whisper on the phone? "Who needs that accent? It's no fun until you see the package," was how she explained it. Sheila is one of the most spirited, interesting people you'll ever meet. "I'm here to have fun, baby" is her catchphrase. In her travels, she managed a graduate degree in physics and an Ivy League MBA. She now consults with Fortune 100 companies on how to optimize employee efficiency by having fun in the workplace. "So you're having a problem with the barking?" She emphatically shook her head no. "Just the opposite, baby," she said, and walked over to the window to examine some drapes. "I don't feel my Bobby Barker and I have the best relationship. He's only interested in me when I'm busy, like all the men in my life. But I'm so much a serious one when I tell you this. It's a gigantic problem." She went on to tell me that Bob would have barking fits when she wouldn't play with him. Her melodrama, phrasing, and a little epiphany I was having caused me to break into laughter. What I had read earlier that day flashed through my mind—"even with proper training this dog will never be quiet," "determined and boisterous"—and yet I felt relieved.

Sheila had somehow made me forget that Bob Barker was in the room. How was this possible, when his barking was all I'd heard on the phone? Why wasn't he barking in the apartment? To this point, Bob had come up for a very civilized meet-and-greet before making his way onto the sofa and puttering around her big living room. He was anything but a nuisance or noisy. In fact, he was church-mouse quiet. Why? The apartment wasn't big enough for the both of them. Even the irreverent Yorkshire terrier was no match for Sheila. Her personality was so demonstrative and loud that Barker couldn't get a bark in edgewise. In a fit of unwanted adaptation, the Yorkshire terrier shut up. The moment Sheila got quiet or on the phone, Bob would start barking up a storm. According to her, he was expressing his displeasure with the relationship, and she may have been right. Bob probably thought something was wrong when things got quiet.

Training entailed teaching Sheila to "share the stage" with her dog. She had to quiet down around Barker and engage him without being so "on" all the time. He couldn't make sense out of Sheila, so he'd step back, attempt to determine his role, and follow the closest thing to a script that he could identify. We practiced having Sheila come home by calmly walking through her front door. Once inside she gave Bob the first crack at being excited to see her. When she made her entrance in a more subdued fashion Bob began to pipe up. I doubt I'll ever have another session like that. I'll never forget it.

Dogs will readily follow scripts and without them attempt to determine appropriate behavior. Although their energies may ramp up quickly and come down slowly, they think their behavior is in line. When a dog jumps on an owner until she's annoyed, getting shoved off in anger will become part of the routine. Next time you come home, hold your ground and don't engage. The dog will eventually realize that jumping up is not producing a worthwhile result and will go back to its business. With enough time, the dog will understand that it is not his job to do this when you arrive.

■ Dogs WILL look to you for cues and clues as to what comes next.

■ Dogs will NOT automatically know what to do or where to go.

Back to the fifteen-minute exercise:

■ Did going into observation mode and departing from the normal routine stress the dog?

■ If so, did he remain stressed?

■ Did the dog redirect onto obsessive or unwanted behavior?

■ Did he stare out the window or begin to bark incessantly?

■ What messages have you conveyed to the dog? For example, are you tense, agitated, or preoccupied?

■ How is the dog to know that he's not the problem?

Studies have indicated that dogs can distinguish between human emotions using their outstanding sense of smell. Even if you two normally celebrate your arrival at home, any worry thereafter could cause a rational animal to wonder if it is the problem. Going forward, try taking some space. After the obligatory "good to see you," settle in and try to sense each other's energy levels and mood.

Remember, dogs communicate and read our signals as instinctually as they breathe, so maybe, just maybe, their behaviors aren't as irrational as they appear to us. Why does a dog chew on a shoe? It's marked with your scent, and it allows the dog to feel close to you; the dog is bored, anxious, lonely, hungry, teething, or underexercised; the dog might be protecting the shoe; or it may resemble one of the dog's toys. There are innumerable possibilities but typically only one main motive per dog.

What did you learn by observing and not readily engaging your dog for fifteen minutes?

■ Your arrival sent him into an excited state (thanks, Detective).

■ He needs to chill out as much as you do.

■ One of you calms down much faster than the other.

■ Without some direction, the dog stays excitable.

There are endless possibilities, but these are the most common. When my dogs first warmed up to me, I thought it was cute: Look at how happy Chiquita is to see me, she loves me so much! The reality is that my border collie/pit mix has a slightly nervous disposition, which is not unusual for the breed. She may be excited and happy to see me, but she's also en route to being stressed. Maybe it's her herding instincts gone a bit awry, or maybe it's part and parcel of living in New York City or being a border collie. Regardless of the reason, I want my dog happy, so an extended celebration routine is not in her best interests or mine.

To get back to the dog's point of view: To best describe the right course of action for you and your dog in a given scenario, consider the dog's personality. In the case of Maya from the last chapter, the difficulty stemmed from human oversight. Rachel knew how playful her dog was and even sensed that Maya's heart was not into training. She knew the deal but understandably lacked the confidence to try training Maya herself. When I first got to her house, I threw a leash on Maya and learned the following by watching her:

1. Maya was playful, physically strong, willful, and sneaky.

2. Maya's ability to concentrate was sound, but her attention span was short.

3. Maya attempted to communicate through play.

4. Maya knew how to perform her commands.

5. Maya was unclear on what was expected from her.

AT WORK, AT REST, AT PLAY

The first couple of points are easy enough—but what does attempting to communicate through play really mean? Maya was clinging to Rachel, trying to engage her in play, because play was Maya's favorite activity. Other dogs might be dying to work with you: Think of a Belgian Malinois performing advanced agility drills, or the sled dogs Roald Amundsen used in a race to become the first person to reach the South Pole (his competitor used Siberian ponies and perished—just saying). These are working dogs. And of course we all know those dogs that just want to chill on the couch: the purebred companion dog for the couch potato. My pit bull, Pacino, wants nothing more than to lie on the couch and be petted. As long as he gets sufficient exercise, I am convinced that dog was born to be in a state of repose. For Chiquita, even relaxing can appear to be a working activity; she constantly checks to make sure everyone's accounted for and in the right place. Maya's default setting was to play for play's sake. Without knowing exactly what she should be doing, Maya was trying to be of service by playing with Rachel. When Rachel pushed her away, Maya's anxiety increased, so she seemed incorrigible even as she tried harder to please Rachel. Using the reward of playing with me to gain Maya's interest, I showed her the fundamentals of a game that called for her to lie on her dog bed. To get her through the learning process, I kept her interest with treats and enthusiasm. Once she knew how to play the "sit on the bed" game, the activity became its own reward. Maya now had a job that gave her structure and confidence. Her anxiety levels dropped, too, which helped her stay on her bed and get some rest.

I mentioned how the activity became its own reward. The activity became its own reward, or was the dog in it for the treats? Well, both. Teaching a kid the basics of hitting a baseball is fairly difficult, but to anyone who has played the game for a minute, there is nothing better than taking batting practice. To a six-year-old, learning the fundamentals of a batting stance—how to keep the head down, swing level, learn the strike zone, and avoid wild pitches—is boring, because all anyone wants to do is swing away and watch the ball fly. One may have to promise ice cream in exchange for fifty swings off the tee, but once those fundamentals are captured, playing the game becomes the reward. The same holds true for dogs.

To get the best out of your dog and play to its strengths, you must take some time to see how your dog behaves in a number of environments while engaged in different activities. From there, you'll be able to glean what motivates your dog and apply that to teaching. Don't worry: In the later chapters, I will provide a list of commands as well as some remedies to common issues. The idea here is to learn to speak some dog, which is a work in progress that will last as long as you and your dog do. Don't worry about getting it all per-

The idea here is to learn to speak some dog, which is a work in progress that will last as long as you and your dog do.

fect, because hopefully you recall that perfectionists never get it quite right.

Assignment: With fresh eyes, just observe your dog's behaviors both on and off the leash, indoors and outdoors, around other people and animals as well as solo. Do your best to observe for a minimum of thirty minutes per environment (listed below) over the course of approximately a week (feel free to keep reading though). Again, this is not intended to be an exact science. There will be some gray areas. For example, a highly alert dog versus an anxious one can be difficult to distinguish.

Environments:

1. Inside the house—both off the leash and on.

2. Outside—in familiar company, on and off the leash (if applicable).

3. Inside the house—around unfamiliar people and animals.

4. Outside—around unfamiliar people and animals.

The environments are pretty self-explanatory. "Other animals" refers to dogs, cats, and wildlife. Having a leash on your dog in the house may be new, so try it out. See if your dog behaves differently, and don't be afraid to use the leash. Do not worry about being too specific in your assessments because you will be using the following five measures, on a scale of 1 to 10, averaged across all environments, to render your verdict:

1. Energy—low, medium, or high (1 to 10). In terms of activity level, does your dog appear lazy, hyper, or somewhere in the middle?

2. Temperament—mellow, average, alert, or anxious (1 to 10). Your dog's general disposition toward the environment: at ease, on guard, curious.

3. Desire to engage—independent (thinks it's a cat), average, or eager (1 to 10). How quick your dog is to interact, play, and learn.

4. Confidence—apprehensive, average, or outgoing (highly confident) (1 to 10).

5. Accelerometer—how quickly does the dog's mood change/escalate (1 to 10). After physical activity, does your dog stay wound up or go right to sleep? When someone rings the doorbell does your dog bark for a few seconds and move on or does it stay amped up?

Before you begin the assignment, take a stab at these numbers right now (the before) using the 1-to-10 scale for energy, temperament, desire to engage, confidence, and accelerometer. Average the numbers out (for example: My dog's energy level across all environments is a 6; its temperament is 7) for a maximum score of 50. I realize that this exercise may feel like an uneducated guess but you'll have another chance as soon as you complete the assignment.

THE EYES HAVE IT

Did you complete your assignment? Maybe you took the initial guess and are in the process of completing the assignment. Have you learned anything about your dog? Did your numbers change between the before and after? Here's a general guide:

Below 10: You should check your dog for a pulse or be more generous with your ratings.

Below 15: Lower numbers can indicate trauma. Shy or disengaged dogs also fall into this range. In general, it's hard to imagine a happy dog with these numbers. If this dog felt a little better, it would begin to act out in less than desirable ways. Not difficult to train but tough to engage. This dog is likely not doing much wrong or even much at all. Needs the Robin Williams character from *Good Will Hunting* to say, "It's not your fault."

16 to 24: The low end of normal. This dog needs more encouragement than most, is likely shy around new people, needs training and socialization. High candidacy for separation anxiety and fear-based behavior. The healthier dogs in this range are usually adults that were always mellow. Dogs in this category are difficult to train as they tend to lose interest quickly, and are tough to get a read on. They are often "poker faces" that need more love and to be made comfortable.

25 to 35: A typically well-balanced dog. Should respond eas-

ily to training. Gives back what it gets. Any difficulties are a reflection of the owner. This range holds the average difficult personality type that is worth the effort, as well as the dog that everyone describes as great.

35 and up: A handful but well worth it. Spirited, not to be easily deterred. If these dogs played football, they would thrive on tough love. Think Bill Parcells or Vince Lombardi as coaches. These are the smart kids who need to be challenged. They can hyper-focus but if you don't keep their attention, those quick minds will find something else more interesting.

By now, you should have a sense as to where your dog fits in, although a dog's profile can change with training and owner input. This is merely the beginning, as we shift our gaze from "what should we do?" to "what are they doing?" As for the numbers you came up with, don't worry about them for now, but do store them in a safe place for later.

A BOX OF ROCKS

When people see a bulldog dragging its owner around or a terrier barking incessantly despite urgings to be quiet, most people will chalk these behaviors up to instincts and breed disposition. These are known characteristics of the breed, so how do people respond to such profiling of their dogs? They limit training with respect to these specific behaviors and end up having walking billboards of breed stereotypes. Bulldog owners who complain about their dog's stubbornness and resistance to learning are often prone to underexercising them. When I suggest sufficient exercise and stimulation as a potential solution to the problem, they shrug and say they heard bulldogs don't need much exercise or interaction. That sucks. When we view certain breed characteristics as shortcomings, learning comes to a halt until the owner is pried open to the possibility that the dog is capable. This may sound kind of obvious, but I would estimate that being prejudicial or rushing to judgment played a factor in over half of the dogs I've trained.

A guy in the dog park used to insist to me that his two-year-old Westie mix named Boomer was "timid" and "dumb as a box of rocks." For the record, there is no way that dog is going to be dumb or void of personality. Why did the man say so? Because Boomer would not come when called. The man illustrated by casually calling Boomer. At that moment, Boomer was fervently digging into dry dirt. Upon hearing his name, Boomer looked up, momentarily surveyed his owner, and went back to his archaeological exploration. Fact: Many dogs in this situation won't look up any faster than a kid in a toy store having a textbook waved at him.

Another couple of callouts, and two angry minutes later, the owner marched toward the dog, now saying "Boomer" with more conviction. His voice didn't get that much louder but deeper and more threatening. By this point, the pack of digging dogs had made progress, and they were taking turns sticking their snouts into the hole. As Boomer's dad made his final approach, Boomer squeezed out a few more seconds of play before getting scooped up. He cringed in his owner's arms as the unhappy man mumbled his equivalent of "bad dog." He stormed back to me, and Boomer's cringing gave way to happiness as he looked at me like a kid who had run into his best friend at the principal's office.

"See what I mean?" the man asked. I didn't. "I give him his time and don't bother the dogs, like some people. I let him do his thing but when I call him nicely, he never comes." He continued this strange defensive pleading: "I'm not one of those jerks who freaks out when their dogs bark or nip each other. I don't bother him. Damn dog." This guy went on complaining about the regulars at the dog park (some of whom, I agreed, were annoying). I mentioned that using a deeper, tense tone of voice was not helpful. He looked at me suspiciously, but to his credit, agreed that marching and pointing at a dog whose head is underground is useless. A minute later, he kissed his dog and told Boomer he loved him. He then said he was a "sucker" and never stayed mad at Boomer for longer than a minute, but Boomer's "stupidity" always wound him up.

Was Boomer a little dumb after all? No way. To my eyes, his personality was social, smart, mature, defiant, and a little sneaky. To his owner, he was a few fries short of a Happy Meal. Polar opposites.

Since we know the owner's rationale for Boomer being intellectually challenged, let's make our case for the dog's genius.

- Social. Dogs that can take turns digging are well socialized, no way around that. The only potential exception is a dog that digs obsessively.

- Smart. Let me count the ways:

1. Boomer knew that hearing his name at the dog park meant "Time to go home," and he was in no rush.

2. The owner's tone told Boomer that he was in trouble, and he made an executive decision to wring out his play-time. I love this dog.

3. The owner had a lot to compete with in the dog park, and Boomer showed great awareness by looking up.

- Mature:

  1. Boomer did not run from his owner. Any dog can be tough to corral at a dog park if they were not trained on this specifically.

  2. Awareness. Boomer's lifting his head upon hearing his name speaks to his maturity.

  3. He was playing with three other dogs and fully coopera-tive.

- Defiant:

  1. Boomer's shift from worried to happy when he saw me is telling. He knew exactly what he was doing the whole time (although this may just be my personal belief).

  2. Many dogs would come running the moment Big Pop-pa's voice dropped half an octave.

  3. Boomer was not intimidated in the least.

- Sneaky. I observed that the dog's cringing was a phony act

Owner's fix: At the park, check in with your dog now and again, and reward it with affection and praise for coming when called. The dog will learn to associate being called with something positive rather than a sure sign that playtime's over.

of remorse that he'd learned to please his owner. I'm admittedly guilty of humanizing this dog on a couple of counts but Boomer had me convinced.

Owner's fix: At the park, check in with your dog now and again, and reward it with affection and praise for coming when called. The dog will learn to associate being called with something positive rather than a sure sign that playtime's over.

Dogs like Boomer are easy to train because they are whip-smart. For us to be good dog owners, we must act like good detectives and be masters of the obvious. To me, Boomer's dad had to use his imagination to make Boomer stupid. Just look at the evidence.

We opened this chapter by citing an example of how an owner sends mixed messages to a dog by trying different tactics before heading back to status quo. This is exactly what Boomer's dad was doing, and the dog rode it out until the old softie returned. The owner would have learned a lot about his dog and found a way to get Boomer to come if he had given him a little more credit. At the very least, he would have been far less upset and a lot more impressed.

As we learn to listen with our eyes, it is up to us to have an open mind that assumes, looks for, and finds a dog's intelligence. Just because a dog's native language and best senses differ from ours does not mean it is incapable of understanding. Just ask Boomer.

CHAPTER 4

A GRAND EXPERIMENT

"The better I get to know men,
the more I find myself loving dogs."
—CHARLES DE GAULLE

S ince we're in the business of teaching people how to speak dog, it is vital to understand how dogs take in information. As the esteemed trainer and veterinarian Dr. Ian Dunbar points out, the dog believes it's training you. The dog wants a piece of food or to be petted, and it sits patiently, with waiting eyes. You say, "Good doggy" and massage its head, and the dog thinks, "Good owner." When a dog that has trained its owner wants to sniff and be petted by a friendly stranger he will sit and wait until the obedient stranger offers a hand, followed by a pet. The dog thinks, "Good stranger, now carry on. Owner, let's keep walking," and off they go.

CAUSE AND EFFECT

Dogs have an outstanding handle on cause and effect because they are tireless practitioners of trial and error. They are continually performing experiments and making learned associations from the results. For example, my dog Pacino is an absolute sucker for affection and will shamelessly seek affection from anyone, anytime, anywhere. In my apartment, he has figured out that when I'm at my desk, I'm typically working. In turn, he won't approach me for a pet when I'm sitting there. When I'm on the couch, he'll take a few shots at me. Sometimes he wins, and sometimes he loses, but he's figured something out. I have a comfortable armchair, and Pacino will accost anyone who gets in that chair for affection. It took me at least a year to figure out why he's at his most tenacious over that chair, but he quickly figured out that he has a high batting average in that spot. Why? Because when I'm in that chair, I'm never working, and I'm not watching television. When I'm occupying that chair, I'm never doing anything in particular so Pacino's pet batting average is at a high there. Moreover, guests tend to gravitate toward that chair, and no guests are turning down Pacino when they first sit. He is also allowed to climb into people's laps on that chair, something he would not typically be allowed to do. To speak to Dunbar's point on the dog training you, it was only after that chair officially got dubbed "the Pacino chair" that I realized what had happened. I got so programmed by my dog that I now make it clear to people who sit in that chair that they are not allowed to ignore Pacino. It is an immutable rule. This evolution took place over the course of a year or more, and I was the last to catch on.

With enough consistency in the results, a voluntary response is produced, and the dog (or the owner) continues to perform the behavior. When conditioned well, we behave consistently, and at some point a voluntary response turns involuntary. Think Pavlov's dogs; think about a dog's reaction as one heads toward the leash closet or when it hears the rustle of dry food being unpacked. The dog's excitement to eat or go for a walk is involuntary. These learned associations and responses work in both directions, though. Should a dog condition itself to be on alert when it hears the rumblings of a garbage truck, there is no conscious control over this response. What compounds these problems is issues the dog picks up from an unwitting owner. I trained a great little Boston terrier down in the Financial District who went ballistic every time a garbage truck passed by. The dog's owner was a super-nice woman from Texas. Dave got her to open up some about her anxieties, and by session's end, she had a breakthrough moment on how much she hated New York City garbage trucks. It was a hysterical purging. It all started on her second day in New York. She'd been ruthlessly hit on by a garbage man. Hailing from Texas, she was too polite to just walk on, so my man probably figured he was getting somewhere. He wasn't her type, plus, it was August, and the stench of hot garbage that permeated the air had nauseated her. Her dog was surely on edge just being in a city for the first time, and although he was probably okay with the smell, the loud engine running and his mommy feeling far less than charmed set off a few of his alarms. These alarms continued ringing whenever a garbage truck went by. It took far less work to decondition the dog once the owner realized that tensing up and suddenly picking up the pace whenever a sanitation truck drove by caused her dog to follow suit.

> *The environment and our every action is either conditioning or deconditioning a dog. Therefore, it is imperative that we become aware of the messages we are sending.*

The environment and our every action is either conditioning or deconditioning a dog. Therefore, it is imperative that we become aware of the messages we are sending.

Dogs jump on our beds, eat off our plates, gnaw on the legs of our furniture, usurp our armchairs, kill rodents, and dig holes for us to beam in amazement at. These behaviors are part of being a dog. Like most creatures, dogs seek out a good time while avoiding pain. Whatever experiment they believe produces a worthwhile result, they will continue to perform, and whatever experiment is met with substandard results, they will abandon. This is how dogs learn, and they reveal this learning to us when they consistently partake in or avoid certain behaviors.

These are all the clues we need to provide them with a happy outcome that works in concert with our needs. For example, if I want my dog to stay in a given place when the doorbell rings, I can teach him to do so by providing affection and a piece of food in connection with performing this action. For both of us, this is a pleasant consequence. Conversely, if your dog chases down a stick you heaved into the woods and proceeds to drop that stick in a sewer, it's a safe bet no one's throwing that stick again—most likely an undesired consequence if your dog has any interest in playing fetch, particularly with that stick. Dogs are quite literal, so your dog may wonder why the game stopped so abruptly; he may also wonder why you didn't climb into the sewer to fetch the stick. The dog is now motivated to get back to playing this game, which is where we come in to provide instruction. With repetition, the dog will realize that fetch requires the stick to remain in play and that the game is a two-way street.

Our aim is to repeat the actions that engender favorable consequences and limit those that lead to negative consequences. Feed the positive, starve the negative.

Dogs are often on the right track or at least in the ballpark. Chiquita is always on alert, which is fine, but I don't want her on red alert. I appreciate the fact that she barks when there is someone at the door, but I did not appreciate it when she acted as if we were under attack. She would frantically pace, growl, and bark wildly, as if screaming, "The British are coming, the British are here!" In the beginning, feeding the positive was not possible. I couldn't stuff a treat in her mouth after the first bark, because she was off to the races. So I ignored her. I did not move a muscle, and she went bananas all by herself. Starve the negative. I also informed friends in advance that I might not get the door for a few minutes. She had to calm down first, and she had to look to me for guidance. The moment she shot a glance in my direction, I would calmly motion for her to come, and have her sit. I did not want to give her a treat because that could have reinforced her reactive behavior. Once I got my friend in the door and Chiquita remained seated, only then would I reward her. Slowly—and it was slow in her case—she caught on, and in time, I was able to reward her after the first few barks. Feed the positive, starve the negative.

> Our aim is to repeat the actions that engender favorable consequences and limit those that lead to negative consequences. Feed the positive, starve the negative.

Side note on the aftermath: I often mention to people to cut their dogs some slack if something is not particularly bothersome. I was never vigilant about enforcing Chiquita's doorbell protocol, and over time, she regressed some. Nowadays, when I answer the door, Chiquita freaks out a little, and then I mildly yell at her to chill out, which does nothing. For me, this is an acceptable amount of chaos and a long way from her days of being stressed out and aggressive whenever she heard the slightest noise outside my door.

When dogs take actions in their world, they quickly learn whether a behavior produces a negative, positive, or neutral outcome. They get balanced in a hurry because dogs warn each other first, then bite, and move on. In dealing with humans, they are navigating far murkier waters. Our world is full of breakable objects with intrinsic value, fearful people, unsoiled belongings, and, most challenging of all, we speak a language that dogs do not intuitively understand. Their world offers a far more effective vantage ground, as nature may be cruel, but it is consistent. Every time a dog investigates a skunk too closely, it pays a price. With us, inconsistencies abound, so learning can be difficult to trust. Dogs would ask us things like "How come I could sleep with you as a puppy and now I can't? Did I do something wrong?" or "How was I supposed to know I got too big to sit in your lap?" As it's been pointed out, a puppy jumping on people is cute, but once it gets big enough, it will get punished for the same behavior. Inconsistent and unfair.

In order to speak dog effectively, we listen with our eyes and respect the fact that we are dealing with a dog that is blessed with an inherent set of behaviors that may not always jibe with our wishes.

From there, we can gain an understanding of the basic principles of dog training and how dogs learn, so we can seamlessly move into commands and socialization before putting it all together.

REINFORCEMENT

Reinforcement is one of the biggest buzzwords in training and, unfortunately, one of the most misunderstood. The business of positive versus negative reinforcement is the stuff of great debate in the world of dog training. Personally, I am gobsmacked that some of the most outspoken dog trainers can so vociferously share their misunderstanding of reinforcement.

In today's dog parlance, positive reinforcement refers to praise or rewards in teaching. Negative reinforcement has become synonymous with dominance-based training or, more accurately, punishing a dog until it gets it right.

Positive reinforcement is commonly believed to encompass training techniques that rely entirely on praise, play, petting, treats, toys, and affection. When a dog misbehaves or performs poorly, the trainer offers continued encouragement and essentially waits for the dog to do it right while passively standing by, waiting to heap praise with a fistful of treats.

Negative reinforcement is considered to involve yanking on collars, hitting dogs, spraying dogs with repellents, yelling, and making mean faces, all in the name of teaching.

These are all inaccurate interpretations of positive and negative reinforcement that have stifled the evolution of dog training. After my short disclaimer, I will offer a simple, factual explanation of the genesis of reinforcement and how it applies to dogs.

DISCLAIMER

In my estimation, nature offers enough deterrents for dogs. A dog that decided to grapple with a porcupine should not come home only to get spanked for having muddy paws. I also believe that punishment-based training can cause negative behaviors to persist when the dog's trainer/ tormentor leaves the room. It is unnecessarily cruel and, in my estimation, ineffective. At best, the dog will behave properly when the abusive person is around. As I once heard, no one would dare train a bear this way. Taking advantage of a dog in a violent manner is inexcusable, sickens me, and makes a strong case for capital punishment.

Dogma aside, here's the deal: You can lead a dog to training, but you can't make it click. If a dog gets sprayed, smacked, and verbally derided for its efforts, it will not be too hip on future training sessions. Trainers who believe in establishing dominance and punishing as the nucleus of their training have not only dogs that hate them but a growing list of conscientious objectors, including me. There is no place for that.

The sad part is that many well-intended positive-based trainers are, regrettably, the most uninformed and indiscriminately critical. Still, they at least aim to make life better for dogs.

That's my disclaimer. If you can stomach the coming pages on operant conditioning, you will have a sense of the psychology behind dog (and people) responsiveness, and at some point, you may have a chance to correct a misinformed trainer. As Josh Billings said, "A dog is the only thing on earth that loves you more than it loves itself," so let's show a little love for our pups by gutting out the next few pages.

OPERANT CONDITIONING

The term "operant conditioning" was coined by B. F. Skinner, a decorated psychologist and behaviorist who decided to pursue psychology after being inspired by the works of none other than Ivan Pavlov. In a 2002 survey of his fellows, Skinner was considered the most profoundly influential psychologist of the twentieth century. Not bad. His statement "the consequences of behavior determine the probability that the behavior will occur again" may well be the calculus of dog training. Although his body of work was largely in the realm of human psychology, his paper simply titled "How to Teach Animals" is an insightful guide into animal learning.

Ironic side note: Skinner built his name through his research on operant conditioning and developed a device called a "cumulative recorder." With this device, he was able to determine that behavior did not depend on the preceding stimulus, as Pavlov had posited, but instead found that behavior hinged upon what happened after the response. He called this operant behavior.

Operant conditioning supposes that learning is based entirely on the rewards and punishments for a given behavior. Via operant conditioning, dogs make an association between a behavior and the consequences of that behavior.

Skinner's work suggested that thoughts and motivations are not reliable in explaining behavior. Rather, we should focus on the external, observable causes of behavior. Through these external factors, we can understand how people acquire the range of behaviors they exhibit on a daily basis. Think of a guy buying flowers to make a good impression on a date. Guys do not buy flowers because they love the smell; they do it based on the potential promise of a reward. Should they receive that reward, the behavior will increase so long as that reward still holds value. When you think of the song "You Don't Bring Me Flowers Anymore," it is clear that the reward-producing behavior has come and gone. Sadly, the potential reward of bringing flowers is no longer of value for the giver. Thus, the behavior of buying flowers has decreased.

Operant conditioning causes behaviors to increase, decrease, or cease depending on the outcome of performing that behavior and the extent to which we value the outcome. What? Behavior increases, decreases, or stops depending on the payoff or lack thereof. For example, a dog learning to relieve itself outside may be doing so to avoid being yelled at or to seek out praise.

It is important to understand the use of the words "positive" and "negative" with regards to punishment and reinforcement. Positive merely means the introduction of a stimulus while negative denotes the removal of a stimulus. Positive and negative have no correlation with good and bad in this context.

KEY COMPONENTS OF OPERANT CONDITIONING

Reinforcement is any occurrence that increases the behavior it follows. There are two kinds, positive and negative.

1. *Positive reinforcement:* Favorable events or outcomes that are presented after the behavior. Guy buys flowers and appreciative flower-loving date throws her arms around him. The behavior is strengthened by her affection. A dog sits when instructed and gets a piece of food. The food is presented after the behavior of sitting.

2. *Negative reinforcement:* The removal of unwanted outcomes or events after the display of behavior. Behaviors are strengthened when the negative reinforcer is removed or avoided altogether. Something unwanted is being subtracted from the equation. In this case, flower guy buys flowers and allergic flower-hating girl sneezes in his face. From this moment on, he buys chocolates for his dates and mother (although he may still get in trouble for trying to gain favor with high-calorie foods). The example that is commonly used is putting on sunscreen to avoid getting burned. The negative reinforcer is the sunburn, which serves as the reminder that strengthens the behavior of applying sunscreen.

These responses are created via the subtraction of something undesirable—sneezing and sunburns, respectively. In the above cases, the negative reinforcers increase a behavior, which is what makes it different from punishment. Punishment is the introduction or removal of a stimulus designed to decrease or weaken the behavior it follows. Again, there are two types:

1. *Positive punishment:* The presentation or introduction of an unfavorable event or outcome to weaken the response it follows. Example: A dog jumps on your guests and gets sprayed with a water bottle.

2. *Negative punishment:* A favorable event or outcome is removed after a behavior occurs. We all know this one: When I play ball in the house, Mom takes the ball away.

Punishment is aimed at weakening or decreasing a particular behavior via the introduction of an unwanted stimulus or the removal of a desired stimulus.

Reinforcement aims to increase wanted behaviors, while punishment is designed to decrease unwanted behaviors.

THE ROAD TO HELL

Intentions are really the thing we have to look at. Are we offering our dogs a chance to do something good or are we attempting to stop them from doing something we don't like? I want my dogs to be calm when I leash them up in the face of their excitement about going outside. I take the leashes off the hook and they begin to act up so I put the leashes back on the hook. Am I doing this to encourage calm or to halt chaos? Putting the leashes away is an example of negative punishment if my aim is to weaken the behavior of my dogs acting unruly. Still, I'm taking an action that anyone would consider reasonable and entirely humane. What makes this act something other than negative reinforcement is a matter of technical definition and a mere tweaking of the act. Let me get to the point. Examine your motives and don't get caught up in the technical definitions. Do I have my dog's best interests in mind or am I acting on my own frustration? Am I guiding my dog to the promised land or am I speeding its path to Hades, hoping it will realize that's no place to be? Drama aside, check your motives and try to offer your dog the swiftest, happiest path to good behavior.

SCHEDULES OF REINFORCEMENT

This is where it gets interesting. In operant conditioning, when and how often a behavior gets reinforced can have a significant influence on the strength and rate of learning or response. A schedule of reinforcement is a set of rules that determine what behaviors will be reinforced, as well as the frequency with which reinforcement occurs. Behaviors will be reinforced all the time, some of the time, or none of the time. Positive reinforcement or negative reinforcement may be used, depending on the circumstance, but, remember, the goal is always to strengthen favorable behavior and increase its likelihood going forward. Remember when I confessed that I got a little lax about Chiquita overreacting when the doorbell rings? I forgot to schedule in my schedule of reinforcement.

Let's take a look at the following reinforcement schedules.

1. *Continuous reinforcement:* Continuous is as it implies—the behavior is continuously reinforced. For example, if you are trying to teach a dog to sit, catching him in the act of sitting, whether or not you asked for it, is cause for rewarding. In the initial stages of learning, continuous reinforcement will make a strong association between the behavior of sitting and the response—for example, getting a reward.

2. *Partial reinforcement:* In keeping with the sit example, partial reinforcement says the dog is rewarded only when you specifically ask it to sit; it would not receive a reward for sitting on its own accord. This is the most common reward schedule with commands and is particularly effective in guarding against "extinction."

EXTINCTION

Extinction occurs when a trained behavior is no longer rewarded or the reward ceases to be rewarding. For a dog, something ventured and nothing gained means it's time to move on. Stick to a schedule of partial reinforcement to safeguard learning from extinction. For example, food and affection typically maintain their value, but the same old toys can get old in a hurry. Vary the rewards and the way they are presented so the dog will keep knowledge of the rewarded behavior handy.

SCHEDULES OF PARTIAL REINFORCEMENT

1. *Fixed ratio:* A behavior is reinforced after a specified number of responses. For example, once my dog can follow the "sit" command with eighty percent success, I will reward the behavior only every third requested "sit." Fixed ratios help to wean dogs off of food rewards and can increase their attention span.

2. *Variable ratio:* A behavior is reinforced after an unpredictable number of responses. Sometimes you win, sometimes you lose. This schedule creates a tremendous response in humans, as evidenced by the popularity of games of chance. In the beginning, consistency in schedules is everything, but once a command is learned, dogs get hyped up by unexpected rewards.

3. *Fixed-interval schedules:* The response is rewarded after a specified amount of time. Useful with dogs when teaching commands like "stay." Fixed intervals allow us to increase the amount of time in which the dog performs the requested behavior.

4. *Variable-interval schedules:* A reward is given after an unpredictable amount of time. This schedule produces a steady response and, like variable ratio, helps to keep a dog's interest.

5. *Shaping:* This is not Skinner's work, but a type of reinforcement dog trainers use. As dogs learn, we expect more from them, but in the beginning, a halfhearted squat can count as a successful "sit." The partial execution or even attempt to perform a command may warrant a reward.

Determining a reward schedule is pretty simple. When teaching something brand-new, continuous reinforcement is great for capturing behaviors. Once the behavior is learned, partial reinforcement refines the lesson, while maintaining the value of the reward.

Things can get humdrum if rewards don't vary some in value, frequency, and presentation. If you don't want your dog to fall into a predictable pattern, then you can't, either. Once a dog understands a command, feel free to reward with different hands, have someone else give the reward (helps with socializing, too!), make the dog wait with anticipation, and occasionally, give it right away. Anything you can think of to keep things fresh works, and, if all goes to plan, you'll be having fun, as well.

DR. FEELGOOD

Why am I so intent on varying the rewards as well as keeping things upbeat and moving? The brain circuitry of humans and dogs, of course. Dopamine is a feel-good neurotransmitter that drives the reward response in humans and most animals. A dog's brain, as well as ours, is extremely attuned to expectations, and when expectations go unmet, dopamine levels fall precipitously. Try telling a kid who ran home from school that he has to wait until tomorrow to play Xbox, and watch the effects of falling dopamine levels.

To understand the link between dopamine and reward circuitry, you have to travel deep within the brain to a place called the nucleus accumbens, where dopamine cells are waiting to fire in anticipation of a reward. Professor Wolfram Schultz at Cambridge University discovered environmental signs that indicate an upcoming reward creates a response in the brain that releases dopamine. These are rewards we know to expect, which transmits dopamine. But guess what releases more dopamine than expected rewards? Unexpected rewards. Surprising rewards and upbeat, unpredictable deliveries can help ward off any downturns in mood. In humans, the drop-off in dopamine for not receiving an expected reward is akin to pain and triggers a small threat response—not exactly a receptive, learning state.

Dopamine cells connect to the prefrontal cortex, which is critical for concentration and learning. Keep expectations positive for the dog, and focus grows accordingly. The connection between dopamine levels and perception is believed to be the reason that happier people experience improved mental performance and increased problem-solving abilities. I personally believe this is also true for dogs, although their prefrontal cortex, in relation to brain size, is much smaller than ours.

To recap: Vary the rewards, and deliver them at expected and unexpected times. Keep the vibe light, positive, and varied so you'll have a supercharged dog to work with. Once some learning is in place, use the power of variable ratio and interval reinforcement schedules so a dog can bask in the element of surprise.

As a dog gains proficiency in training, we can up the ante to reward only the best responses based on our criteria. An underperforming dog will soon realize what it takes and up his game.

CHAPTER 5

GIVE THEM WHAT THEY WANT

"He listens to his trainer real good.
He just doesn't listen to me. I still can't get him to do nothing."
—EVANDER HOLYFIELD ON HIS AKITA,
WHO HAD COMPLETED OBEDIENCE TRAINING
WITH A PROFESSIONAL TRAINER

I'm not against telling a dog no, though there are some people out there who would scalp me for making such a declaration. Many contemporary trainers espouse a purely affirmative delivery system in training. While it's an admirable notion, I have yet to see it work effectively. That said, I do believe that delivery of the big N-O makes all the difference, and how it is best said depends on the dog. Yet another reason to listen with our eyes, because you are responsible for knowing the inherent temperament of your dog, not the trainer you hired. For me, I know Pacino could outlast any drill sergeant's diatribe, while Chiquita's feelings would get hurt if she were exposed to the same admonishment.

Finding the right working tone requires one to always pay close attention to a dog's immediate reaction. For example, Pacino takes a moment to consider (not process) the information you've sent him, regardless of tone; Chiquita hears a tone and immediately reacts to it. Even a stern "Pacino, come!" is met with a pause and a look that says, "What's in this for me?" "Pacino, off the couch!" is followed by the canine version of a "whatever" look. He always moves but takes his sweet time. Chiquita, on the other hand, I can't speak to that way, because her eyes will dart nervously, her tail will lower, and she will withdraw. "Off the couch" needs to be delivered very evenly. I first learned how sensitive she is to tone by watching her reaction to my neighbors yelling at each other. With physical things, though, she's anything but sensitive. She's built like a mixture of a torpedo and a seal and could wrestle all day and have nothing but fun, but if my tone is a little off, she wants to withdraw.

For the record, my dogs are allowed on the couch when I invite them, but once in a while they'll take a shot and show up unannounced. When Chiquita was young and I was teaching her the "off" command, I would lead her to her bed and have her sit there, or I would take her to her toys and encourage her to grab one. Telling her "off" was not enough, because she would pace and bide her time until she thought it might be okay to be on the couch. Now she understands what her options are when the couch is not available. The "off" command is not communicating that she's unwanted. This is a hugely important point in teaching, so I am shouting the following two sentences: *Do not tell your dog what you don't want it to do. Tell your dog what you want it to do.*

Never begin a sentence with "I don't want my dog to____ [insert annoying behavior/habit here]." You will get nowhere very slowly.

"I don't want my dog to freak out when strangers come in." "I don't want my dog to relieve himself on the carpet." "I don't want my dog to dig holes in the backyard."

When someone asks you, "What do you want the dog to do?" "Anything but _____" or "Not _____" is not an answer. When I ask people, "What do you want the dog to do?" I get what they don't want the dog to do a minimum of three times, followed by a vapid stare and eventually a thin smile that yields to an "Aha! I get it." At this point, they usually admit that they learn more slowly than their dogs, and I thank them for their honesty, give them a hug, and say, "I think we had a breakthrough." Dogs cannot learn the behavior you want them to perform if you don't know what it is!

BALANCING ACTS

To get our dogs to do the things we want them to do, we must understand what motivates them to behave. At the top of the list, dogs want to spend time with their owners. They want praise, affection, downtime, and playtime. Once a dog's fundamental needs are met, these are its primary wishes. And when these wishes are met, we have a balanced dog.

The term "balanced dog" is thrown around a lot, and its meaning has had bleach poured all over it. It has come to mean, more or less, that a dog has a friendly disposition, but that is incomplete. I believe the genesis of this phrase comes from the expression "A balanced dog has titles on both ends." When a show dog qualifies for a championship at a conformation show, a "Ch" (short for champion) is added as a prefix to its registered name. A conformation show (aka a dog show) is a competition to see which dog best "conforms" to the breed and embodies its essence. The same prefix designation holds true for dogs crowned the victors of performance championships, such as endorsed flyball and agility competitions. Should the dog go on to win other titles outside of the main conformation and performance competitions, or gain certification such as water rescue dog, these titles are added as suffixes to its name, hence "titles on both ends" (of the name).

The expression came into vogue in the general dog public as debate stirred around purebred breeding, with the correct claim that overbreeding led to "imbalanced dogs."

The reality is that a balanced dog has balanced owners who provide a balanced life for the dog (yes, that's three in one sentence). This means a routine: a sound diet, steady exercise, mental stimulation, structure, and, of course, affection. Cesar Millan can also be credited with popularizing the expression and his definition is darn good: To him, a balanced dog is comfortable in its own skin and in any environment. It is secure in its role in the family, has activities that it can perform with others or alone, and is largely void of nervous urgency, desperation, and the need for continuous attention.

The reality is that a balanced dog has balanced owners who provide a balanced life for the dog (yes, that's three in one sentence).

When we begin training, it is helpful if the dog is balanced or at least in a balanced place. This means that prior to training your dog has received some exercise, affection, reward-based interaction, and a chance to play with a coveted toy or two, and is now eager for reward-based affection. In the long haul, the toys and treats are just part of the repertoire of a top-flight dog parent. The dog enjoys them because they came from you, and its wish to partake in training is in order to engage in structured work/play. Once a dog understands what training is all about, receiving your praise will mean the world to it, though praise in and of itself is not something dogs connect to instinctually. Dogs come to associate praise as a good thing because it is often followed by treats and affection.

GLORIOUS FOOD

The ultimate reward for most dogs is food, and every dog has some food drive. We use food as motivation because it works and works well. Feeding a dog its meals as a reward in training spurs on learning, and being hand-fed by an owner is an intimate touch. I typically prefer food as a reward because toys are difficult to negotiate with during training. It takes any dog but a second to down a piece of kibble, while wresting a chew toy from a dog mid-lesson can be disruptive. Kibble is a term that means to "grind or divide into particles or pellets," but in dog vernacular it refers to prepared dry food, which I don't recommend. When I use the term "kibble," I intend to refer to any healthy food (turkey is my favorite) that can be broken into small, easily consumed bites.

A well-socialized dog may be motivated to learn from interaction alone, but we're not afraid to make life easy, so we add the element of food. Even if a dog has lower food drive than most, training makes the food more interesting.

NO NEGOTIATIONS

Food is a tool in training. It is not the reason that your dog accepts training. We carefully avoid getting into the business of bribing. When dogs are off performing their experiments and we call them, we don't wave food in order for them to join us. They make the choice to partake. We don't use food to change behavior; rather, dogs choose to engage in behavior modification games (such as training) in which food is involved as a reward. We lure the dog in by offering it the chance to socialize and play with us, and, hey, guess what? It just so happens there's some food in it. As mentioned earlier, once the fundamentals of a game are mastered, the activity becomes the reward. In my experience, dogs get to a place where training or performing the command itself is pleasurable. Once this juncture is reached, food can be weaned out altogether or may still be used as an accelerant in teaching.

■ Portion control: Dogs will work for barely a lick of food. I mean this. Without exception, people overfeed their dogs when training. Replace a handful of kibble for a single shred of turkey or something similar and further reward the dog with your time, attention, interest, and affection.

■ Affection control: For dogs that aren't particularly food driven, affection often works. Praise and affection should be meted out in a fashion that doesn't make the dog too excitable.

THE SPICE OF LIFE

There are reward systems supported by trainers that remind me of cable television plans. When a dog does a basic thing well, offer a basic reward; for more challenging tasks, serve up a silver or gold reward . . . all the way up to platinum, I'd guess. I don't think this is necessary, though I understand that a dog's mojo may match what it's working for. Exhibiting portion control keeps dogs interested as does varying the treats; just make sure there's nothing too cumbersome or tough to chew on. When you're teaching something new, new treats can help. Special occasions also call for special actions. Despite my insistence on portion and even affection control, when your dog loses the training wheels and does something truly laudable, have special treats on hand to mark the occasion.

SAY IT LIKE YOU'D WANT TO HEAR IT

Clear, crisp, and calm is the aim. Deliver praise and appreciation evenly, consistently, and enthusiastically, but don't be over-the-top. Don't fill the air with talk. Commands and teaching are being delivered to an animal with astounding senses, and it will zone in on everything until it can parse out relevant from useless information. Prattling on makes this difficult to impossible. Remember my run-on sentence from earlier? Here it is again: "Wait, come, look at me, pay attention, good boy, good dog baby, now come, sit down, you can do it, that's it, come on come on puppy dog booby baby you can do it, sit, sit, sit down already, just sit, like this, sit, sit, sit." When people garble or speak in whole sentences, dogs are now being asked to pick out key words. I tend to drone in a happy way, "Gooood boooyyy-hhh" (or "giiirrrrlll"), but I don't notably raise my voice. Drawling the words also allows me to transition from one activity to the next and keep the "good vibrations" going. Some trainers can be highly effective while remaining stoic and near silent, but I think that makes it more challenging. The one thing that does distract dogs is the "irrationally exuberant" approach. The loud evangelical sorts can slow the learning and set the bar awfully high for themselves. When the zest begins to wane, the dog will wonder what it did wrong, and anything short of a parade will sound like disappointment.

You may recall that I used an "all-in" level of enthusiasm with Maya. I understand that this somewhat contradicts what I've just said. Again, I preach guidelines not gospel. These are general rules to which there are exceptions. Maya's previous experiences with instruction had dulled her to learning and I surmised that she would need to be drawn into a game. That said, guidelines and general rules are not absolutes but do apply in the large majority of cases.

It is important to develop a training style with a basic understanding of these principles and an ability to use them. As you'll read below in "The Zen of Training," I encourage owners to be more boisterous and demonstrative in issuing praise or treats. Being clear, crisp, and calm as a foundational style gives us something to deviate from as we develop our own training style in accordance with our dog.

THE ZEN OF TRAINING

Once a dog gets on board with training and the owner feels the winds of momentum blowing sweetly against their back, things can get fun. To this point we've been diligent in becoming good-postured trainers who deliver our messages calmly, clearly, and crisply. We exercise portion control with aplomb. We are steadfast in making sure our dog is in a good working environment and not distracted by any superfluous movement or talk. What's next? It's time to let our hair down and let things get fluffy. "Keep it fluffy" is something I often say to my clients. People concentrate so hard on their dog's every move that they end up looking like our national security is at stake. It should be fun, light, and fluffy. Once in the groove, hand out treats with gusto. As I said before, once you're under way and the dog understands what's in it for them, enthusiasm and interactivity can be the "rocket fuel" of training. Between the legs, behind the back, extra treats for extra-good work. Keeping it fluffy staves off boredom; looking stern and acting bored do not bode well for the dog (or you).

Learning should be a structured playtime for you and your dog. This is your time together, and play you must. Dogs will associate play with learning, and keeping the spirit of play in the air is a panacea for humans and a boon for a dog's demeanor. Through training, we build trust and gain our dog's confidence. A dog's innate sense of curiosity is forged, fostered, and channeled, and through training, a bona fide value system is constructed. I said "value system." That sounds good and is yet another phrase that gets thrown around. What does it mean in relation to dogs? A dog's domesticated purpose is to work, and training becomes a job that can engender a genuine sense of accomplishment. Dogs come to value their time with you, learning, performing commands, and partaking in their role as family member. That said, sitting, staying, heeling, and coming are not exactly what dogs were brought on this earth to do. Please understand that they may find following basic commands unnatural at first, if not a little irritating. For a dog to do its best, it must sense your pleasure. When it does, a dog will recognize its value, and its temperament will shift. Tug-of-war, fetch, and physical games assimilate easily into a dog's psyche, while modern-day learning must be cultivated. Rewards in the form of owner enthusiasm, affection, and some treats are all integral components of the process. Once dogs understand the value proposition of performing commands, they will do so with zeal, and it will be good times all the way around. When training is going well, reward your dog in a dizzying array of fashions. "Dizzying" may be pushing it, but don't be a somnambulist handing out the goodies in a solemn state. You can always go back to clear, calm, and crisp, but sometimes having your dog jump up to take the treat, or chase you for it, is just what the doctor ordered. The idea is to make learning fun by "keeping it fluffy."

COMMUNICATION

So how do dogs best communicate? We know they have outstanding olfactory systems, but dogs are visual animals that do their very best to understand us. They don't learn words as we do; rather, they come to associate an image or action with a sound and respond accordingly. This may be obvious, yet we continually fail them by being unclear in our communication. "Mushing" is the term I use for people who are inexplicit with their voice and/or body when dealing with a dog. They often slur their words together while simultaneously throwing up indistinct hand signals; hence mushing. Culprits of mushing, interestingly enough, often have vague or unrealistic expectations of what they want the dog to do.

What we say and what dogs hear can be very different. Think of dogs as hyper-literal animals. From both a visual and an auditory standpoint, what they see and hear is what they get. Aurally speaking, their need for precision is greater than the most frustrating automated phone menu. "Come," "C'mere," "Come here," "Fido, come on," "Come on," "Come on, boy/girl," "Come, boy/girl," "Here," "Here, doggy," and so forth are all different to a dog's ear.

Given that they learn visually, hand gestures and body language must be definitive or they will be misinterpreted. Communicating with dogs is one of the few things in life that is truly black and white. When you get the hang of being extremely coherent in voice and body, it is also quite enjoyable. The best possible way I know to illustrate this is to tell you the story of Mr. Roboto.

THE TALE OF MR. ROBOTO

A vicuña-colored year-old golden retriever/Irish setter mix named Oliver, or Ollie as he was called, was part of a great family comprised of four individual humans: an inked-up teenage daughter, a quiet son of seventeen, an outspoken matriarch, and a super-nice, easygoing husband to go with one confused and hyperactive Ollie. Everyone had his or her own way of doing things, and each person's approach to the dog could not have been more dissimilar. Ollie knew how to sit well enough, and I began there; escorting the family out to the backyard to have them practice the heeling technique (which I will cover in Chapter 7, "Command Central"). To make it extremely simple, the heeling technique is basically a dynamic walk/sit exercise that involves walking with your dog a few clear steps before coming to a stop. You then instruct the dog to sit alongside you, with a hand signal and the word "heel," before resuming again. When the exercise is done well, it's not quite balletic but is pretty graceful. When it's not done well, it's a herky-jerky, asynchronous practice where all parties are completely out of step.

The two kids had the most interaction with Ollie, so they went first. It was a disaster. It wasn't even close, and Ollie immediately became frustrated. I shot Dave a look that said, "This is going to be a long day."

Then the outspoken mom went and somehow was worse than the kids. Finally, it was the dad's turn. I was feeling pretty hopeless as one low-key guy slowly stepped up to the plate. I handed him the leash and wanted to cover my eyes. In his day-to-day, he spent very little time with Ollie, but he was willing to give it a shot. And then . . . something amazing happened.

Ollie followed his lead as if they'd been doing it for years. Dave and I started cracking up as we both caught on to what was happening. Dave quipped, "Rhythmless nation," and he was right. The father was nervous to perform in front of his family, which made him literally uptight. He walked more upright than I thought possible. Each one of his steps was the exact distance as the step prior, and he progressed in a long, bounding, and rigid march. His hand gestures were so stiff that they looked comical but proved expert. His daughter said, "You should see him dance," but Dad got it right. He became the model, and the other family members did their best to imitate him. The results were notably better. In their initial efforts, Ollie was picking up on everything: For example, the son walked with his head down and his hand in his pocket—this was the same hand that held the reward, and predictably, Ollie fixated on the pocket at times. There were so many misleading cues being sent to Oliver, until Dad came along and showed us all up. If I ever doubt how clear one needs to be with dogs, I will always remember the man we dubbed "Mr. Roboto." Now let's break it down:

Mr. Roboto had mastered the art of separation: separate and distinct steps, hand gestures, and movements. When he first attempted the hand signal he was not doing anything other than standing erect and moving his open palm upward from his belt to his chest. "Right in the strike zone," as we say. When Dad took his three steps, he wasn't flailing, swaggering, or sauntering; he was forward marching. When he stopped, it was sharp. He deliberately moved the treat from one hand to the other to reward Oliver and flawlessly repeated the steps. It was something to behold.

A dog's sensitivity to physical gestures must be respected. Any habit or tic will likely gain some meaning to a dog. Whenever I train, I notice that the most difficult thing for owners to master is their own body. In the case of Oliver, the two kids were the walking cautionary tales. The son was a very slim, soft-spoken high school senior with loose arms and a loping gait. By the time he finished his three steps and turned to Oliver, his limbs were all over

A dog's sensitivity to physical gestures must be respected. Any habit or tic will likely gain some meaning to a dog. Whenever I train, I notice that the most difficult thing for owners to master is their own body.

the place and his head always ended up turned away from Oliver. He would then mumble, "Heel," to no effect. With practice, he did just as poorly but began to punctuate his third step with a dramatic half-spin so he could actually face the dog before looking away again and mumbling, "Heel."

The daughter walked hard, and her left arm swung up in an aggressive gait. She, too, had an affinity for looking down and away. After three steps she turned to Oliver and shouted, "Oliver, heel!" Ollie looked shocked. By her third effort, Oliver was used to it and began to jump and prance as if someone had asked him to wrestle. When the command is clean and definitive, the movement should be subtle, and even the kids improved eventually when they imitated their father.

The other takeaway from the story of Mr. Roboto is the need for consistency. When you have a dog that appears to listen to a certain person, it is very often the case that this person is the most consistent in voice and body. In rare instances, that person is a Mr. Roboto sort, but most of the time, he or she has paid close attention to what the dog previously responded to and replicated it.

Our variations in voice and body language can cause a dog to appear as if it has not learned the command. In such cases the dog has picked up on certain cues and associated them with the command but does not always receive these same needed cues when being taught. Ultimately, it is up to us to find the needed degree of consistency.

CHAPTER 6

TOOLS, TERMS, AND TRAINING

"Here, gentlemen, a dog teaches us a lesson in humanity."

—NAPOLEON BONAPARTE,

WHO WAS SAVED BY HIS DOG

AFTER FALLING OVERBOARD HIS SHIP

(HE COULD NOT SWIM)

Every dog owner needs to have an understanding of some basic dog training techniques and their application. The most challenging task for a dog is to connect words to actions, so we begin with markers or marking words.

MARKERS

And you thought dogs got to do all the marking? Since dogs do not have an instinctual association with verbal praise or punishment, it must be taught. Markers allow dogs to connect to and define words when they are paired to a particular action. The marker word is the word we choose to say the moment before we give a reward.

After a dog executes a command I consistently say, "All right!" and give the dog a treat. It will know what "All right!" means. The mark of saying "All right!" builds a bridge between the act of executing upon the command and the receipt of a treat. There is always a little downtime between the dog's positive action and the reward; the marker creates a continuum between the positive action and the delivery of the reward. The fact that it comes before the treat makes it the most important link in this little daisy chain of requests ("Doggy, sit"), action (sitting), marker ("All right!"), and outcome (treat goes into waiting mouth).

Delivering the treat right after saying the marker word(s) is essential. Using markers in conjunction with rewards will cultivate a dog's vocabulary and act as a homing device to the right behavior.

MAKING THE MARKER COUNT

Should I say "all right" to my dog when the dog is outside the context of marking, the word's meaning and impact will be diluted. Needless to say, phrases like "good dog" are easy to overuse, and can completely nullify the intended use of a marking word or phrase. The way I coo the rather generic "goooood giiirrrllll" (or "boy") is reserved solely for training. Remember, to a dog, a straight "good dog" sounds completely different than "gooood dooogggg."

When it's well timed, a marker acts as the click of a camera shutter for the dog. Dogs are visual learners and will snap a picture in their mind of what they were doing the moment the marker hit home. With repetition, a bitmap of images forms and crystallizes around the proper behaviors.

Dogs are visual learners and will snap a picture in their mind of what they were doing the moment the marker hit home.

Warnings are a type of marker that can let a dog know it's missing the mark, so to speak. When a dog veers off course, a quick "ehh-ehh" signifies to the dog that the reward does not come along this path. The warning builds a bridge from "the land of the lost" to the "promised land," taking the dog from being off course to on.

After saying the marking word, always give the treat. Should you serve up a warning and the dog catches on and comes correct, make sure you state the marker before dispensing the treat. Do not forget that for a marker to be productive, the word, phrase, or sound must contain a unique, dedicated meaning. My friend Kokomo uses "boo-yaa" as a marker word. When he says, "Doggy, sit," and the dog sits, Kokomo says, "Boo-yaa!" to mark the behavior and create a bridge to the reward. The dog receives the treat and the circle is closed. The marker also signifies the end of the repetition. Feel free to be creative in making your own marker.

When things don't go smoothly: "Doggy, come." The dog veers off course and I warn, "ehh-ehh," to build a bridge to the right behavior. When the dog gets back on course and starts heading my way, I can use another bridge word, like "yesss," to offer a positive hint. With practice, the dog will understand "yesss" to mean that he's en route to a reward and "ehh-ehh" to mean that he's moving away from the reward.

Common mistake: delivering the marker, warning, or treat too late. To quote B. F. Skinner, "To be effective a reinforcement must be given almost simultaneously with the desired behavior; a delay of even one second destroys much of the effect. This means that offering food in the usual way is likely to be ineffective; it is not fast enough." That is a little dramatic, but it is the reason we use markers in the first place or we'd really have to rush to deliver the treat. The marker buys you some needed time. Delays of even a few seconds may render the point moot, so be ready to repeat in order to get it right.

TO CLICK OR NOT TO CLICK

The clicker has gained popularity in recent years, and for good reason. A clicker is a small handheld device that makes a—you guessed it—clicking sound. It's a pretty sharp sound that reminds me of a metronome and it acts as a marker. For some, having the clicker in hand helps with timing: In one hand, I'm holding the treat, and in the other, a clicker. The moment the dog executes the command, I click and offer the reward. Is it better than your voice? If it improves timing, then it may well be.

Given how I've harped on timing and rapidly closing windows of learning, using a clicker to close the gap between command, mark, and reward can be very useful. For those of us who get caught up in the excitement of the moment ("Such a good doggy, you did so good, who's my doggy?") or those who can't hide their frustration, the discreet click removes the element of emotion and provides an unmistakable marker for the dog.

If clickers can improve our timing in dispensing markers and remove the fallibilities in voice, what could be wrong? Nothing terribly wrong, but it's one more thing that you need to hold. You've got a treat in one hand, maybe a leash in the other, possibly a pouch on your hip, you're administering instruction while watching the dog, and now you've got to remember to click. It may be inconvenient for some. I get satisfaction from personally communicating with the dog, and I believe our voices can deepen the connection, but that's just my belief. I've used a clicker before and consider it an individual choice.

One potential drawback to the clicker is the need to offer a reward every time you click. That is nonnegotiable or the clicker will lose its value. Naturally, my voice is something I use all the time with my dogs, so weaning them off rewards is easier because the dog will not automatically associate my voice with a reward.

Whether you use a clicker or a voice to mark, the learning process is the same. At first the sound has no value or meaning to the dog. When you begin to click and dispense the reward, it comes to symbolize a sign that reads "Treats just ahead." This is established with repetition, and when the dog is conditioned to it, the clicker is what's known as "charged." Just like we don't overuse our marking words, make sure not to dilute the value of the clicker by using it in lieu of snapping to your favorite song. One person told me that she used her clicker compulsively when she worked from home, often snapping it off thirty to forty times a minute as she sat at her computer. She then wondered why it wasn't effective with the dog.

LURING

Dogs are nature's homage to the success of trial and error. As dogs get a handle on markers, they will build a compendium of favorable behaviors and constantly rifle through their archives in search of behaviors that produce reward. Once a strong base is laid and a sound vocabulary is developed, their demeanor and overall behavior become not only more predictable but generally better. It takes some work to get there, but once a dog's learning engine is on, it will aim to please and look for ways to do so. Until this engine light goes on, we have to do our best to draw them in, and this means luring.

Luring is the introduction of a reward in order to draw in (or lure) the dog into training. Placing a piece of food by a dog's nose is usually good enough to garner interest, and this is exactly what luring is intended to do. Certainly, it has a purpose, but I caution owners against overusing the simple technique. Dogs that have been "overlured" can come to balk at anything unless they see a treat. To use luring effectively, a dog's interest must be piqued.

LURING IN TRAINING

When training, it is a good idea to hold the treat out at your side. Initially, the dog will eye the treat before looking to your eyes for instructions on how to earn it. When I teach a puppy to come by holding a piece of food and repeating the word "come," he will surely do as told, but it's difficult to cull exactly what he has learned. Is the dog associating anything with the word "come," or is he following his nose? Typically, a bit of both. With repetition, he will get the right message. Where luring truly works wonders is with the "sit" and "down" commands. If you hold a small piece of food by a dog's nose and simply raise the food, the dog's eyes will follow it. Quadrupeds, when looking directly overhead, will naturally go into a sitting position. In this case, even if the dog is following its nose and not your instructions, it will catch on just the same. The food goes overhead, and when the dog looks, it will surely sit. After the dog sits, please be sure to mark the behavior with "Boo-yaa!" or similar and dispense the treat.

PURSUIT AND CAPTURE

To help our dogs learn, we can augment their never-ending treasure hunts for rewards by "capturing" the behavior we seek. For example, if you're trying to teach your dog to sit and you catch the dog in the act of sitting, offer a reward. It is an example of continuous reinforcement: We reward the act even when we did not request it, in order to speed learning. Should you catch your dog lying on his back with his legs straight out you can reward the behavior, and the dog may learn a neat trick. From there, give the trick a name like "dead," and soon enough, the dog will perform a pretty sound imitation of a stiff.

SHAPING: CLOSE AND YOU STILL GET THE CIGAR

As mentioned in schedules of reinforcement, shaping a behavior is to reward the dog's actions that come close but don't perfectly fulfill the requirements. Your dog paid attention to you and went into lying position instead of sitting as requested. Shaping says you would reward the behavior and give the dog credit for trying. As the dog learns, these "close but no cigar" efforts are rewarded. Shaping says we give full credit for the partial execution of a command, but I often take it a step further by rewarding initial eye contact.

Remember, "The eyes have it." When I begin to teach, I am often standing and holding a treat in my hand with my arm extended away from my body. When a dog is willing to look away from a treat in favor of looking at me, I know we're on the right track. Before I attempt much of anything, I will wait until we are eye to eye, because I want to guide the dog to the treat. I may have to wait for a dog to exhaust all avenues first: Staring at the treat, jumping, whimpering, running in circles, and a whole host of inaccurate reward-seeking behaviors. Eventually the dog will finally look to me and say with his eyes, "What can I do to get that?"

To an outside observer, it looks like I'm trying to cast some sort of spell on the dog by looking him down. I'm not. The dog wants the reward, and he's trying to perform for it. He's on the case like an old gumshoe and will look to me for clues. Once he does this, we start building a relationship. It is my job to guide him to and through the command so eye contact is the first step and I'm happy to reward it. How long eye contact can be maintained varies, but if we can lock eyes for just a few seconds, I deliver the reward. This is the first piece of shaping.

Rosie and myself during *Dogs in the City* filming.
(Credit—CBS Dogs in the City)

My first dog, Zack.
(Credit—Justin Silver)

Swimming with Ollie.
(Credit—Justin Silver)

With my mom and Zoe.
(Credit—Brian Friedman)

Dave and I with Gustav and Kennedy. *(Credit—Brian Friedman)*

The Language of Dogs family: Nicole, Dave, Laura, myself, and Barb.

(Credit—Brian Friedman)

Funny for Fido "Comics stand up for homeless animals"—pictures from our annual charity event, which I started in 2006. The dogs and shelters we support along with comedians Colin Quinn, Dave Attell, Judah Friedlander, Amy Schumer, Robert Kelly, and Rachel Feinstein.

(Credit—Brian Friedman and Heidi Kikel)

When *Dogs in the City* premiered, it made the cover of *The New York Times*'s Arts Section. What an honor. *(Credit—Heather Wines)*

Pacino, Chiquita, Buster, Taxi, and myself walking the carpet.
(Credit—CBS Dogs in the City)

The incredible *Dogs in the City* crew on lunch break.
(Credit—Justin Silver)

Walking my pack on the West Side Highway. *(Credit—Brian Friedman)*

One of my favorite scenes from *Dogs in the City.* Gathering my buddies to help a troubled dog, Oso, overcome a fear of men. It felt very manly for all involved. *(Credit—CBS Dogs in the City)*

Some of my favorite clients, Great Danes Harlo, River,

A day on the farm with Pacino, Sadie, Shadow, and Buster. (Credit—Justin Silver)

"Look, Ma, I caught a pit bull!" Camping in Ojai, CA.

My kids with tails in Santa Monica, CA.
From left: Buna, Cowboy, Dexter, Pacino, and Bailey.
Mural by Kristel Lerman. *(Credit—Christian Mack)*

With Chiquita and Pacino.

(Credit—Brian Friedman)

Chelsea Piers with Pacino.

(Credit—Brian Friedman)

Using the "sit" command as an example, let's go through it. I say the dog's name as I hold a treat out at my side. The dog looks to the food and I wait until his eyes are on mine. Ideally, we get a little stare-down going. I reward eye contact and ready another treat. This time, I raise the food up past the dog's nose and toward my eyes as I say, "Sit." The dog gets to look at the food and my eyes, a no-lose situation. Should the dog only approximate sitting, I mark that action with "Gooood boooyy," and I give the reward. Eventually, these attempts will produce a successful sit.

Allowable margins of error are part of being a good parent to your child, and it's no different with dogs. The beauty of teaching with shaping is that it creates a paradigm where "close" can win you the cigar.

With a target behavior in mind, shaping allows the dog to be led in the right direction and encouraged. Our own miscues are expressed through the dog, so when we can't find a good reason to reward the dog, we're doing something wrong. It's easy to figuratively shake our heads until the working partner (the dog) in the relationship does something right. However, when we take responsibility for playing the lead role in this game of charades, then it becomes a team sport.

I want my dog to come to me when he's called, now what's the plan? Will I require the dog to come and sit on my feet, or will it suffice if he gets within arm's length? How long is the dog required to stay if he comes to me? I must know this and plan with the individual dog in mind. For example, my observation of high-energy dogs has taught me that getting eye contact is one thing and keeping it another. Many high-energy dogs concentrate intensely in short bursts so I won't sweat the small stuff. Dogs on the shy side may be intimidated by your physical presence, so turning sideways and squatting down makes you more approachable. When a dog is nervous or preoccupied, I will practice some patience and tolerance and give it some time to work through its discomfort.

THEORY, MEET PRACTICE

In the real world, dogs jump, run in circles, and do all sorts of things, especially when you're trying to teach them. Do not give up. Ignore the dog until he does something right. Rethink what good behavior means: The dog stops being nuts for a moment—reward it. There is no need to get into a bribing scenario where we try to distract the dog from its state of distraction. Unless you've determined that you are attempting to teach your dog in a competitive environment, paying the dog no mind and waiting to reward is still training. By "competitive environment," I mean an area where there are loads of stimuli that would have genuine value to the dog. In the case of Maya, the second trainer attempted to train her outside a dog run, and had no chance. Picking a suitable environment or figuring out the best motivator is guesswork until it becomes intuitive.

Once I have a clear picture of what I am teaching and a basic plan to get there, establishing a basis for success is next. When things are not coming along, I will backtrack. Each basic step of a command should be performed soundly and consistently before moving on. "Soundly and consistently" means an eighty percent success rate.

Eighty percent success rates are the goal. In order for your dog to be an A student, it needs to earn a B-minus.

Owners are often tempted to speed the process along or quit when they see the finish line. They speed the process by nearly performing the command for the dog and are ready to move on the moment their dog shows any sign of willing participation. Should I physically pull my dog over and stuff a treat in his mouth, he will not know the "come" command but will come to expect treats for being pulled. We have to teach until the dog is truly eighty percent of the way there or this omission will come back to bite us you know where. The dogs may think, "All I have to do is let this ding-dong pull me around while he shouts 'come,' and I get free food. I like this game." Listen with your eyes, assess your dog's level of interest, and wait until something right happens. Reward the good and move incrementally down the path. Once things are under way, raise the stakes by having the dog work a little harder for each subsequent reward.

LINKING

To determine and understand your dog's window of learning, conduct a little experiment: How long can you lock eyes with your dog? This is roughly how long you have to get your point across. Since dogs are domesticated to take cues from our eyes, they have a great facility to improve upon this. In my experience, even the most anxious dogs will calm down when their powers of concentration are directed onto our eyes.

With shaping, we form a nexus between steps of the process while steps themselves are the links. The comprehensive "come" command is linked by a few steps: stepping away from the dog a proposed distance, turning to the dog, getting its attention, calling the dog with "come," the dog coming to you at a desired pace, having it stop and then sit at a set point. These steps are all linked, and dogs are visual, so they will associate our cues to link the actions into a sequence. Teaching the steps is a matter of creating cues. How much refining each step calls for is personal. For me, the "come" command requires the dog to come to me but not necessarily sit. Others want the dog to walk, not run, to them, come to a full sit, and be willing to stay put. Getting a dog to walk, not sprint, can be accomplished by marking the word "slow" when the dog slows down; even an "ehh-ehh" will naturally slow a dog. The dog forms relationships between actions and sequences, then connects the dots that produce a reward. The most complex routines of agility dogs are testimony to the power of sound linking.

Breaking down a command into individual components allows one to reward the right responses and correct the wrong. When a dog performs four of six steps correctly, how can it learn where it went wrong? By defining the individual steps of the complete sequence. Teach the steps in order, as each step is a cue to the next and a confirmation or mark of the prior action. It is fine to teach either forward or backward, but never out of sequence, or the links will break.

Once a dog learns a command, it will be punctuated with a word like "come." There can be more than one word: "Come, Fido" or "Slow, sit, stay." Repeating words like "come" is useless until the dog knows what the words mean. Only after the dog has demonstrated eighty percent efficacy will the word stamp the sequence for the dog. In teaching the individual steps, your physical cues, followed by the dog's physical actions, are the real indicators of learning. This is what makes hand signals so effective. A definitive wave over will create an association with the word "come" a lot faster than the sole vocalization of a command. The first connection is usually made to the hand signal, not the word, so we link a hand wave to the word "come."

A definitive wave over will create an association with the word "come" a lot faster than the sole vocalization of a command.

PROOFING

The successful execution of a command does not necessarily mean a dog has it down pat. How you play in practice and how you play in the game can be very different, and this is where I see the most flummoxed dog owners. A dog learns to sit in the kitchen with a certain person, and it knows how to do just that: sit in the kitchen for that person. It does not automatically make the connection to "sit" as a concept. Dogs act locally and aren't so great about thinking globally. What a dog learns in one place may not hold up in another. "Yeah, I understand what you're saying, but you should see how good she is with so-and-so in the den" is the cri de coeur of many dissatisfied dog owners. How do you get a dog to take its learning on the road? Practice, practice, practice.

Remember how a dog can take a snapshot and create a bitmap in its head? When a dog is instructed to perform a command in the park that is learned in the living room, it might notice there are no sofas in the park and ignore you. It might even be laughing at you on the inside, wondering how you confused a park with your living room. It will recollect body language and tone of voice down to the minutiae and incorporate those details in constructing visual snapshots. It is in this picture that the dog understands the command, and outside this context, it may be at a loss.

To proof (or prove) the behavior, it is necessary to teach the same commands in a number of places, ideally with different people. Locales that are loaded with distractions are not ideal at first. Reward the dog regularly and increase the degree of difficulty as it gains mastery over the new environments. Buy some new treats and give them with vim and verve.

AVERSION AND CORRECTIONS

"Aversion" and "corrections" are two more words that push the buttons of controversy in the world of dog training. There are outspoken pundits who decry the application of what has been dubbed "aversion-based training." I won't engage this controversy but will tell you that an "aversive" is an action that intends to remove a behavior. An abusive aversive would be yanking a dog's leash and making a mean face while saying, "Cut that out," as is pushing a dog's nose into its own feces. Conversely, if a dog is getting wound up and is "pinning"—or staring down another dog with visibly bad intentions—a sharp "hey" and the offer of an alternative also provide an aversive. The alternative could be a reward, a command, or any activity that will redirect the dog away from subpar behaviors. Aversives can be effective in dealing with dogs that begin to fixate or obsess on things. Physical aversives can be abusive, and they also tend to ramp up a dog's stress levels when the idea is to bring them down. Aversives have become synonymous with abuse and punishment, and that is not what they mean.

A correction is exactly what we all know it to mean. In the vernacular of dog training, it has come to mean something abusive or negative, although it did not start out that way. If someone is walking a dog and intends to go in a different direction from the dog, the pull on the leash that the dog feels is a correction. It may be course correction, but it is a correction nonetheless. When the same dog beelines to get nose-to-nose with a pile of garbage and the owner spots shards of broken glass, and pulls the dog away, she has just corrected the dog.

When corrections turn stupid is when the dog is being corrected for something it did not know in the first place. We can't correct something that was never learned; we can only teach it. From an evolutionary perspective, a dog's very survival is dependent upon being of value to us. Too many trainers forget this simple fact and proceed to take out their incompetence on a dog that will lose interest and begin to avoid learning altogether. I once read that corrections are not for mistakes, and I could not agree more. Once a dog becomes well versed in a command or activity, then corrections take on the tenor of refinement as you lead the dog back to a correct behavior. These corrections lead the dog to a reward.

Dogs absolutely need to comprehend the correction, or, before you know it, you'll be correcting the dog for not knowing the correction. The dog needs to understand both the action and the correction. Cold. When I am attempting to maintain eye contact while holding a treat, a dog's hungry eyes may veer away from mine and to the food. When I say "ehh-ehh," that constitutes a correction that tells the dog "eyes on me." I am telling the dog that the trail to the reward is getting cold and I want to lead him back to warm, warmer, hot, and "Boo-yaa," the treat. Corrections are best when paired with praise. My "ehh-ehh" to a dog straying from a reward should be followed by a positive marker once he's back on course.

Teaching and learning from a dog that is truly engaged is one of life's joys, and when this is realized, the activity becomes the reward. For both of you.

CHAPTER 7

COMMAND CENTRAL

"He who wishes to be obeyed must know how to command."
—NICCOLÒ MACHIAVELLI

Welcome to the hub of all learning. By now you have come a long way, having toiled through some heavy lifting in the previous chapter. You are ready to teach your dog. What do dog trainers do, by and large? They solve problems and teach commands. Your dog is soiling the furniture? It will learn how to go outside via commands. For every problem, there is a command waiting to tackle it. I will restate the key terms and provide a list of all the basic commands you'll need to have in your repertoire. You will need to remember:

Partial reinforcement: We reward the dog for performing the command only when we ask.

Rewards: Come in the form of treats, toys, and/or praise.

Shaping: This is where "close" gets you the cigar. The owner must have the end result in mind and reward the dog when it approximates the desired behavior.

Linking: Breaking down a command into individual components. Always teach in order.

Fixed-ratio schedule: A type of partial reinforcement. Once the command is mastered, we reward only after a fixed number of repetitions are completed.

Marking: Using words and signals as a bridge between the action of performing the command and the outcome, or reward. The marker word is what one says before dispensing the reward, such as "Boo-yah!"

Proofing: We proof, or prove, the behavior by practicing the command in more challenging environments and situations, such as on walks, in parks, and around other people and animals.

Eighty percent rule: Do not add criteria to a command or change the reward schedule until the dog can perform the command with eighty percent consistency. Each phase of a command should be learned with this rule in mind before moving on.

Strike zone: The space in which we communicate hand signals to our dog. This zone is between our belt line and chest. The hand should be about a foot away from the body.

Your dog's vocabulary is equivalent to how many words or signals it understands. Bring a leash, rewards, a pocketful of patience, and a good mood.

THE "LOOK" COMMAND

It is one thing to call a dog's name and get some of its attention and another to call the dog to action. Bribing is a common error in calling a dog: "Woo-hoo, Fido, look what I have here" or "Hey, Sparky, check this out," is not the idea. Just the name, ma'am, and the word "look." The "look" command is designed to get a dog's attention.

With reward in hand, start by calling the dog's name, followed by "look" to get its full attention. Keep the treat out at your side and wait for the dog's eyes to move off the treat and on to yours, then reward. Practice until the dog can give a minimum of three seconds of eye contact eighty percent of the time.

Shaping
The dog will typically notice the reward and stare at it. Should the dog make eye contact even for a split second when it hears "look," reward.

Cheat
If all eyes are on the reward and not on you, move the hand that's holding the treat to your nose. The leash is also helpful to keep a distracted dog in proximity.

■ When Justin first holds the treat out to the side, Chiquita is all eyes on the prize.

■ Chiquita recovers quickly by giving Justin her attention upon hearing the word "look."

■ With Pacino and Kennedy jealously looking on, Chiquita is rewarded for holding a few seconds of eye contact.

Proofing

1. Switch the hand you hold the treats in.

2. Little by little, turn away from the dog and let it come find you for eye contact.

3. At a full 180 degree turn, say, "Look," and see if the dog will walk around to face you.

4. Move a few yards away, turn around and perform the "look" command once more.

5. Practice "look" while on walks or while playing. During fetch, pick up the ball, say, "Look," and hold eye contact for a few seconds before tossing the ball.

THE GENTLE COMMAND

The gentle command teaches dogs how to accept rewards like a lady or gentleman. Owners who have "chompy" dogs often dangle rewards a few inches away from the mouth out of fear. Although understandable, this only encourages the dog to lunge and chomp. Teaching a gentle mouth is necessary for good etiquette.

Casually hold a small reward in a closed fist and allow the dog to smell it. The dog may mouth your hand, which can be corrected by saying "ehh-ehh!" or "ouch!" to trigger bite inhibition. Puppies will naturally release a play bite from a dog that lets out a shriek. Should the dog attempt to paw at your hand, keep your fist close to its nose until a softer approach is attempted. For the less courageous, place the reward in the palm of an open hand.

Marking

The dog may lick your hand, wiggle its snout into your fist, or delicately nibble at the hand. Say, "Gentle," open the hand, and when the dog takes the reward in a softer fashion, mark with "nice" or a similar word of praise.

THE ALMIGHTY SIT

A dog must be able to sit on command before you can effectively teach the heeling technique or the "stay" command. It is also a good rule of etiquette to have a dog sit when being introduced to a stranger, and in some circumstances, it may keep a dog safe. Its applications are endless.

Place a treat in your flat palm, facing skyward, and secure it with your thumb. Turn your palm over to allow the dog to smell the reward and then, with the palm skyward again, raise your hand a few inches, directly above the dog's head. When dogs have to look straight overhead, they naturally go into the seated position. Should the dog sit, reward; if not, be patient and try again. An open palm facing and moving upward is the common hand signal for the "sit" command.

■ Justin holds the treat in the strike zone as Shamon's nose gains interest. Notice how his eyes stay on Justin for instruction.

■ By moving the treat higher and over Shamon's head, he is forced to look up, causing him to move into a sitting position.

■ Justin maintains his posture and the position of the treat as Shamon comes to a full sit.

■ A smiling Justin serves up the goodies to the working Shamon.

■ Standing tall and at a distance where the dog can clearly see Justin, Justin illustrates the hand signal for "sit." Palm up and arm in front of his body, the hand moves through the strike zone to just below his chest.

Shaping

Reward anything that looks like sitting. If the dog sits and gets right back up, try to reward while the dog is still in the seated position.

Cheat

A little push on the butt can move things along and challenged dogs respond better to "sit" when on a leash.

Capture

Whether or not the command was requested, capture the behavior by rewarding the dog in the act of sitting. Should you catch your dog in the act of sitting, say, "Sit" and reward the dog.

Advanced

Step a foot away and prompt the dog to sit solely by signaling with a flat, upward palm moving through the strike zone. Try using the word "sit" without the hand signal. Just before you reward, mark with a word of encouragement.

Proofing

1. Practice from a distance.

2. Practice alternating hands to signal with.

3. Increase the length of time the dog stays in a sit before releasing.

4. Have your dog sit when you put the leash on, before you let him outside, before you throw the ball during fetch, etc.

5. Practice on walks, in parks, and in "real-life" situations, rewarding only the best performances before moving to a variable-ratio (random rewarding) schedule. If you remembered "variable ratio," you've read too closely.

THE "COME" COMMAND

"Come" is among the most important commands, because it can save a dog's life. It is the command that can stop a dog from chasing a squirrel into the street. Starting at a distance of a few feet, wave and call the dog to you with the word "come." This is the one command where giving up your good posture is worthwhile. Feel free to bend and wave, squat and summon, or lay and pray; just get your dog to learn this vital recall. The waving over can be demonstrative or even exaggerated at first. Clap, whistle, or dance without sacrificing the integrity of your hand signal (which is not so easy). When your dog arrives, it's time for rewards and affection. Don't be shy.

Shuffle back a few more feet and use a marking word when the dog arrives. Repeat this by going backward in a straight line, and with each repetition, say, "Come."

Shaping

Meet the dog halfway or if it stops coming to you, reward it just the same. Should the dog veer off course or attempt to walk past you, intercept the dog and reward.

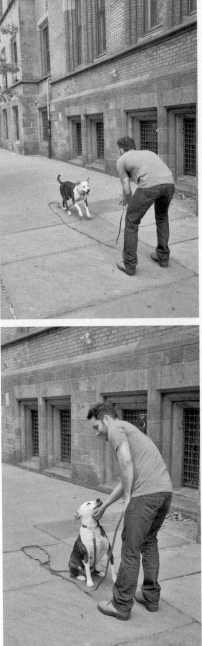

■ Command Come 1—On a long training lead, Justin beckons Chiquita to "come." In the beginning, your enthusiasm will come in handy.

■ Command Come 2—Chiquita comes with happy abandon.

■ Command Come 3—Chiquita stops, sits, and is greeted with affection.

Luring

At first, use squeaky toys, treats, whatever it takes to get the dog to come toward you. The message is "If you come when called, it's the greatest thing in the world."

Cheat

Use a long training lead to guide the dog toward you.

Capture

Use opportunities to capture the command by saying "come" in situations where the dog would head your way automatically—as you pour food into a bowl, squeeze a new toy, or take the leash off the doorknob.

Advanced

After the hand signal/"come" is mastered, try whistling and clapping. When your dog comes to you, add the "sit" command and delay the reward, so your dog learns to sit patiently.

Note

The "come" command is one that needs to be worked quite a bit. Before upping the degree of difficulty, make sure the eighty percent mastery rule is more like ninety percent.

Proofing

With two people standing far apart, call the dog and have it go back and forth, but make it worthwhile, with treats. Treats can be decreased using a fixed-ratio schedule, so reward the dog only after it has run a couple of laps. For example, the dog runs to Person A, then Person B, then back to Person A before being rewarded.

Play hide-and-seek: Run into different rooms and call "come," only in this version of the game, let the dog find you. With a twenty-foot training leash, practice "come" on walks by allowing the dog to walk ahead of you and harkening it back. Practice in distracting environments: around a few people or other dogs (dog parks may be the ultimate proving ground; just ask Boomer's dad), wherever the environment vies for a dog's attention.

THE "STAY" COMMAND

In the beginning, eye contact is essential for this command, as most dogs need a line of sight to you in order to stay put. A longer leash, like the twenty-foot one you used for the "come" command, is helpful.

With the dog facing you, say, "Look" to get eye contact, and make the "halt!" or "stop in the name of love" gesture about a foot away from your dog's snout. Take a small step back, then return to the original position and reward, provided the dog stays put. Always return to the dog and wait a beat before rewarding.

1. Use the hand signal and say, "Stay" before stepping back.

2. Take additional steps away from the dog before coming back. Extend the number of steps and increase the time with each additional pass.

■ Dave has a thirty-foot training lead on all 125 pounds of Dexter in the distracting environs of the Venice Beach boardwalk. Dave signals Dexter to "sit."

■ Dave gives Dexter a very clear sign to "stay."

■ Backing up, Dave repeats the hand signal in case Dexter had any plans of wandering.

■ Dave ups the ante on Dexter as he begins to walk around him.

■ Dave is all the way behind Dexter, who is staying put. Extra bonus points to Dexter for craning his neck around to seek out any further instruction.

■ Dexter is so good that even the leash running up his back doesn't move him out of position.

■ Dave gives Dexter some earned praise for a job well done.

3. Use a release word to signify the end of a series of repetitions. Work toward getting to the end of that twenty-foot leash.

Cheat

Should the dog stray from the "stay" spot, the leash can be helpful to move the dog back to a starting position. Reward liberally in the beginning, and you should be able to get a few steps back with eighty percent success fairly quickly.

Shaping

Should the dog take a step or two and stop, reward.

Proofing and Advanced

Mix it up by walking away at different angles and add time by having your dog wait before releasing. Walk in a complete circle around the dog and if you're indoors, go into other rooms or out the front door. Add more challenging environments and serve treats only to well-executed stays.

Practice throwing balls or placing food on the ground and have the dog stay until you issue the release command. This is known as the "wait" command, and it can be an excellent tool to curb compulsive behaviors and teach patience. For example: A good practice is to have a dog sit and wait before you place its food bowl on the floor.

THE "DOWN" COMMAND

The "down" command is the same as "lie down." With your dog sitting, hold a reward in a loose fist, facing down. Place your fist in front of the dog's nose and make sure the dog can smell the treat. Slowly lower your hand to the floor, and the dog's head should lower to follow your hand. If it does, say, "Down." Should your hand reach the floor, slowly slide it away from the dog. With practice, the dog will lower its body to follow the reward and go all the way into the lying position. If this happens say, "Down," mark with "Good," and reward with a treat. If he doesn't lie down, reward him with a treat for bending his elbows or lowering himself. With each repetition require the dog go a little lower before rewarding. In the photos, you will see me performing this command on a dog that knows the command pretty well.

Shaping
It's very important to reward the dog should it bend at the elbows or lower itself in any way.

Cheating
Use the leash to guide the dog down (do not pull or force), and it may lie down.

Marking
The moment the dog lies down, use a marking word and reward.

■ Shamon is sitting attentively as Justin shows him the reward. A rare instance where good posture is compromised.

■ Justin allows Shamon to smell what he's working for.

■ Justin lowers the treat and Shamon follows his nose.

■ With Shamon fully in the down position, Justin opens his hand and dispenses with the treat.

- Justin is more upright here, holding the treat, palm down, as his hand signal sends Shamon to the down position.

- Shamon, being a model dog (get it?), willingly follows the command.

- Justin gives Shamon a treat while he is still in the down position.

Proofing

1. Use distance by starting a few feet away and advance to ten feet or more.

2. Practice this outdoors, preferably around other people and dogs.

3. Move to a fixed-ratio schedule and reward only after a few successful repetitions.

4. Pair the "down" command with "stay."

Many commands can be paired; for example, "sit" and "stay" are commonly used together, as are "down" and "stay."

THE HEELING TECHNIQUE

When a dog sits alongside its owner, it is considered to be in the heeling position. Should a dog excitedly run up to investigate someone, saying "heel" will cue the dog to come back alongside its owner and sit. The heeling technique is simple in spirit but the most complex command to teach and practice. I will offer an abbreviated explanation so owners can get started. In order to learn how to heel, the dog needs to have mastered the "sit" command.

One big difference between heeling and other commands is that the dog is at your side, not in front of you. The dog will need to adjust to this, as well as a decrease in eye contact. When delivering the treat, you need to turn only your upper body toward the dog.

■ Shamon is angled slightly behind Justin and giving great eye contact. Justin rotates his trunk and gives the hand signal right in the strike zone (between the belt and chest). Note Justin's feet facing forward and though he's shortened the leash, there is still a touch of slack in it.

■ An upright Justin strides forward, confident that Shamon will follow. Many beginners keep looking back to check on their dogs and this can disrupt the rhythm.

■ Readying for the big stop just a step away.

■ Shamon's eye contact is legendary as Justin turns to give the hand signal. Shamon will be sitting slightly behind Justin and Justin's feet will be facing forward as they ready for another rep.

1. With a treat in one hand and the dog on a leash in the other, have the dog sit alongside of you. Choose your left or right side. This is the heeling position.

2. Let the dog sniff the treat and keep about a foot of slack on the leash.

3. Say, "Heel," take three strides with the dog, and come to a definitive stop.

4. Once stopped, quickly move your treat hand upward (a short version of the "sit" signal), turn your upper body to the dog, and say, "Sit."

5. If the dog sits alongside you, reward.

6. Repeat steps 3 through 5 for a set of three repetitions: Each rep is saying "heel," taking three distinct steps and stopping.

The trick with heeling is fluidity. Miscues happen when an owner raises his hand before stopping and making eye contact. In this case, the dog can't see the signal. People with a lot of body language in their gait often send out too many signals. Mr. Roboto was perfect because his strict movements were so clear. Once the dog catches on, the movements become much more rhythmic.

Cheat
The dog may be tempted to face you head-on; use the leash to stop the dog from walking around.

Shaping

The main idea of heeling is to get the dog seated alongside you, so reward any effort that comes close. The goal of the "heel" command is for a dog to walk with you, then sit alongside you when you stop.

Advanced

Once the dog is following the "heel" with eighty percent accuracy, you can phase out the "sit" command. Try calling the dog to you by saying, "Heel." Add a visual cue by slapping the thigh you want the dog to heel beside.

Proofing

Practice heeling from both your left and right side. Move to a fixed-ratio schedule so the dog has to perform three perfect reps before being rewarded. Practice in the house and around people, as well as in competitive environments. Practice this command on walks! It helps to eliminate pulling, teaches a dog to walk alongside its handler, and sends the message, "When I walk, you walk, when I stop, you sit."

THE "OUT" COMMAND

This command teaches the dog to leave. With a reward in hand, lure your dog to the doorway of a room you want it to leave. Point toward the desired area you wish for the dog to go and say, "Out," as a reward is tossed in that direction. As the dog progresses, wait a few moments before throwing the reward.

Cheat
Use a leash to guide the dog into the other room or outside.

Shaping
Should the dog leave and come right back, take it back out and reward. If the dog leaves but heads in the wrong direction, reward just the same.

Capturing
Use areas where your dog typically wants to go, such as the backyard, and say, "Out" as it bolts out the door.

Marking
As the dog crosses the threshold into the target area and takes his reward, say, "Good" or a marker of your choice.

Proofing
Practicing this at other people's homes is hugely helpful, as the dog will understand that "out" is a request to leave, not necessarily a destination.

THE "GO TO" COMMAND

This command teaches the dog to go to a specific place, such as a dog bed or crate. To help with learning, teach one destination at a time.

With your dog on a leash, start a few steps away from the destination and point to the spot. Wait a moment and say, "Go to spot." Walk the dog to the destination and use the "sit" command, followed by a reward and "stay." As the dog gains proficiency, say, "Go to spot," and only walk the dog halfway. Continue to point at the destination, and phase out the "sit" command.

Cheat
Use treats and toys to lure the dog to the destination as well as to keep her there. A leash can be helpful in guiding the dog to the spot.

Marking
Use a marking word when the dog's front paws hit home, followed by the reward.

Shaping
If the dog is heading there but veers off, enthusiastically assist in the final steps and be sure to reward good efforts. Shaping is everything in this case, so please reward all attempts the dog makes to head toward the target spot.

Note
In the beginning, a flat mat or towel works better than anything that has to be climbed into.

Proofing
Practice the command from a distance and even try with the dog in a different room. Increase the time and use a fixed-interval schedule, rewarding the dog after a specified amount of time before releasing. A dog that performs this command without a line of sight on its owners has it down.

THE "OFF" COMMAND

"Off" tells the dog to get off your bed or couch, or to remove his head from the toilet. It is also used in situations where the dog may put its paws on a person or up on a table. "Off" is similar to "down," but they are still separate commands. Many people say "down" when they want the dog to get "off" so please note the difference.

Point to the place where you'd prefer the dog to be—for example, a spot on the floor that is near the sofa that the dog hopped on. Say, "Off" as the dog moves from the sofa and delay the reward until the dog moves onto the desired spot and offers eye contact.

Luring

Use treats and toys to lure the dog from the place you don't want it to be. Point your finger and lure the dog in the direction of where you want it to go. Reward.

Cheating

Use the leash to guide the dog off the "no-no" spot and onto the desired area. Don't yank, and be sure the dog doesn't have to jump from a height that could injure it. Even if your dog found its way onto your kitchen counters, don't practice there.

Proofing

Practice in applicable circumstances, such as getting off the kitchen table or your bed. Practice issuing the command from a distance.

The "Up In" Command

This is to teach a dog to hop up on the couch or a bench or into your car, or to go into its crate. Whether to use "up" or "in" is a matter of preference and self-explanatory (I don't want a dog in my sofa). Using a couch as the example: Let the dog smell the reward and lure it to the couch. With a treat in hand, point to the couch. Using the leash, lead the dog to the edge of the couch, point, and say, "Up." If the dog does not go up, place its front paws on the couch. If that's ineffectual, try to lure the dog by throwing a treat or squeaky toy on the couch. As you advance, "up" should be said in tandem with pointing at the sofa. Delay the reward until the dog hops up.

Capture and Marking

The dog may jump up on its own, and continuous reinforcement will help to capture the behavior. Say, "Up" as it jumps, and mark with "good," followed by a reward.

Note

Some dogs are intimidated to go up ramps or stairs. Enthusiastically jogging up a set of stairs with the dog can help to overcome its fear. Your encouragement is vital as both a motivator and a distractor.

Proofing

Practice this on things a dog is not crazy about going up or into, like the vet or groomer's table and bathtub. Pair the "up" and "off" commands so the dog learns them together. Decrease the rewards by having the dog perform a few "ups" and "offs" before being rewarded. I taught this by having my dogs jump in and out of the empty bathtub. When it finally came time to introduce them to the water, getting into the tub was not intimidating.

THE "LEAVE IT" COMMAND

This command teaches dogs not to pursue things like your shoes, food, garbage on the street, and the like. I use the word "object" to refer to anything the dog values, whether it is an object or food.

To begin, place an object of low value, like an old toy that your dog is over, on the floor. With the dog on leash, walk past the object at a distance of a few feet. When the dog looks at the object, say the dog's name and give the "look" command in an excited way. When the dog looks at you, say, "Leave it," and offer some praise as you two amble past the toy. Reward.

Marking
Whenever the dog walks by an object of desire, offer praise with a marking word immediately followed by a reward.

Shaping
Reward the dog for minor investigating before it moves on or even if it stops to look but does not touch.

Proofing
Increase the desirability of the object and move the game off leash. Delay the reward by having the dog go by the object more than once. Walk the dog past the object using "leave it," then the "sit" command.

THE "DROP IT" COMMAND

This command teaches a dog to drop an object from its mouth. It all starts by giving the dog a toy, ball, or tug rope. This object should be something the dog enjoys holding but will give up without a major fight.

Place your hand under the dog's mouth and gently hold the end of the object, but do not tug. Introduce the reward by allowing the dog to see and smell it. When the dog opens its mouth to take the reward, it will release the object. Upon release, say, "Drop it." The physical cue is an open hand that says, "Give it here."

As the dog advances, delay the reward and work until saying "drop it" and opening your hand simultaneously is understood. Try not showing the reward and see if the dog will drop it.

Shaping

Reward any considerations the dog makes, such as loosening its grip or if it appears to be considering letting go.

Marking

Dogs tend to open their mouths quickly to snatch the reward, so marking the action with a word of praise is a matter of timing.

Proofing

Play tug-of-war with your dog and periodically have it drop the tug toy. Pair the "drop it" command with "sit." When the dog lets go of the object and sits, be sure to give high praise and certainly reward by giving the toy back and continuing to play. Once this command is understood, phase out treats.

THE "TAKE IT" COMMAND

The "take it" or "pick it up" command can be practiced by placing a desirable object a few feet away and having the dog "stay" before it can be picked up. Since we want the dog to take the object, teaching this is easy when the object is something the dog likes.

Marking
When the dog picks it up, mark with a word of praise and reward.

Shaping
Reward the dog for smelling or mouthing the object.

Cheat
Soaking an object in chicken stock makes most anything desirable to the dog. Use the leash to keep the dog in the "stay" position.

Proofing and Advanced
Use a fixed-interval schedule by extending the length of time the dog holds the object. Try having it run with the object in its mouth. Take a walk with the dog carrying the object in its mouth, and use rewards for continued holding. Practice with a variety of neutral objects, such as sticks, tennis balls, keys, and newspapers. Try naming the object as you mark it. "Pick up newspaper."

The Exchange Game
"Take it" and "drop it" are easy to explain but difficult for dogs to master. The best way is to work them together by playing this easy

game: Use two objects that are equally high in value, such as two squeaky new balls. Give the dog one ball and let it play for a minute before surprising him with the other. To make the exchange, use the "drop it" and "sit" commands. When you hand over the new ball, say, "Take it." Pick up the other ball and repeat this exchange until the dog gets the hang of it.

Did you get all of that? I realize it's quite a bit of information. Training a dog properly may seem daunting at first, but if you keep your eyes open, the dog will provide dozens of opportunities for you on a daily basis. Do your best to incorporate commands as part of the daily interaction with your dog. This is truly how the dog learns, as repetition is the mother of skill for both dog and owner.

CHAPTER 8

JUST TO BE SOCIAL

"Dogs love company. They place it first in their short list of needs."
—J. R. ACKERLEY

A human's world is alien to a dog. Despite their ever-growing domesticated abilities, dogs do not come equipped with a handbook of how things operate in our realm. It is entirely incumbent upon us to teach them the ways of our world.

We cannot assume that it is normal for a dog to feel a leash around his neck; nor can we expect him to lose his desire to bark, mark territory, chew, and aggressively bite things he perceives as threats to his physical well-being. These are standard-issue canine behaviors that dogs instinctively perform. Unfortunately, a dog that bites can invoke society to institute a death penalty, and even lesser offenses can send owners scurrying for the nearest dog shelter. In such cases, a more socially acceptable response (by our standards, of course) for these behaviors is always missing, and this is our failure. Imagine what someone would look like eating linguine if no one ever showed them how to use utensils. It would not be pretty. The reality with dogs is far worse than a lack of teaching; it is our initial acceptance of these behaviors that can lead to a dog's untimely demise. Owners everywhere slough off a biting puppy as cute—we call it "nipping," which even sounds cute. As the dog grows and its bite becomes worse than its nip, it is now labeled a "bad dog." Too often we treat problematic behaviors by attempting to wait them out. When these problems are not automatically outgrown, people treat dogs like lemons from a used-car lot and send them to the proverbial scrap heap.

Most dogs in shelters are roughly six to eighteen months old, adolescent dogs that were not properly socialized as puppies. Dogs enter adolescence at roughly six months, and depending on the size of the breed, the teen years can last until the dog is three years old. Adolescence is typically marked by some notable changes in behavior, and too often owners who have failed to socialize their dog properly end up deeming the dog's issues intractable.

EXPECTATIONS

My mother will attest to the fact that it took a lot of work and no fewer than a couple of years for me to master "please" and "thank you," despite the fact that we both speak English. She taught me with a gentle nudge and other times not so subtly. Despite the deliberate message and reminders, it took a few years before I was consistently willing to use these words in my interactions. By contrast, a dog can learn what to chew on, where to chew it, and even when to chew in a few hours, and with steady practice can master a behavior in days.

The point is that a dog learns "please" and "thank you" far faster than I did but it still requires consistent work.

Dogs are social animals and quick studies that are very willing to learn manners, etiquettes, and protocols of behavior that make them all but perfect ladies and gentlemen in a domestic setting. If we do not take advantage of these abilities, dogs will be left to fend for themselves and try to determine what works on their own.

The dictionary defines socialization as "a continuing process whereby an individual acquires a personal identity and learns the norms, values, behavior, and social skills appropriate to his or her social position." The operable word is "continuing." Although a dog is most teachable when it's a puppy, even older dogs can shed their skin and refine their identity. Most training books are puppy-centric, rendering dogs over four months of age seemingly hopeless and unable to learn. This is not so. Similar principles apply, and though an older dog may be less malleable, all dogs can learn. In fact, the majority of dogs I train are adult dogs. Giving up on teaching dogs that have reached adolescence or adulthood is not only without basis but serves to multiply the shelter problem.

Dogs were not made for life in the city, but over one million dogs can be found thriving in the bustle of New York City alone. A dog misbehaving on an elevator is going to get called out in a hurry, but the good news is that same dog will get daily opportunities to amend and learn new behaviors. It will get conditioned to this environment by being commanded to sit during elevator rides, and will become desensitized to strangers coming and going in cramped quarters. Socialization is an ongoing process of conditioning and desensitization. We condition the response with commands and desensitize our dogs through incremen-

Socialization is an ongoing process of conditioning and desensitization.

tal exposure to triggering stimuli in order to form positive associations.

For every behavioral problem there is a command that can fix it, but behind every behavioral problem is a socialization problem. Somewhere along the way, a dog did not learn how to properly interact with the environment. How do these problems manifest? They manifest every time a dog performs an experiment in its environment and makes associations based upon the results. This happens any number of times per day. If the sample size is small and the lone or few "snapshots" are negative, a negative association has been formed, and when this happens around the wrong thing, "Houston, we've got a problem."

SIMON SAYS

I worked with a two-year-old golden retriever named Simon who had difficulties around children. No great surprise, as it's been said that dogs are less comfortable around men, children, and strangers. This means their greatest comfort level is around familiar women. Though I feel the same way, life involves more than spending time with women familiar to us.

Simon is the consummate happy golden retriever who became skittish and defensive when he got around children. He would send out a few warning barks and growl while backing up. It may have looked threatening enough, but it was clearly not an aggression problem. Simon simply had a very vocal desire not to engage kids. I asked the owner about her experience with Simon around children. When he was a pup, she refused to take the dog around children because she thought the neighborhood kids were too rough with other dogs. She may have been right but avoidance is rarely an advisable solution. When Simon was a little under a year old, she let her neighbor's son play with him, and apparently, like a good neighbor, the kid flew a toy plane into the dog's face and poked him in the eye. The dog scampered away, and the kid made flying sounds with his toy plane as he approached the dog again. Guess what the dog did? He growled and backed away. What did Simon's owner do after that? She scolded the dog for growling and, from that moment on, avoided kids.

What was she doing when the dog first met the kid? She was chatting with her neighbor. Why? Because Simon had no particular reaction to kids from a safe distance and was now mostly grown. To that point, concern for her dog had her avoiding kids, and now she decided to turn Simon loose solely because he had reached physical maturity. Apparently, no introduction would be necessary, because Simon was a good dog.

In the wake of this incident, Simon's owner now avoided children to the point where she would cross the street rather than walk past them. Simon's interactions with children were limited to a trial sample of one. This solitary encounter resulted in a poke in the eye, and from this point on, Simon would be quick to avoid anyone who was not tall enough to ride a roller coaster. Reasonable to me. Every time she crossed the street to steer clear of those dang kids, Simon's owner was sending a message that children posed a threat. Socialization is a "continuing process," and she continually conditioned the dog to consider children dangerous. Simon was socialized to be wary of children, and the lone incident was proof enough for the dog. Had Simon ever been cornered by an unsuspecting child, he may well have bitten. Although it would have been purely a defensive maneuver, it could have not only injured a child but also endangered the dog's life. The solution? Get some kids that are not armed with toy planes around the dog.

Over the course of a day, we carefully guided Simon through the land of children to gradually reduce his fear response. At first I brought Simon in the vicinity of kids and waited for his growl before redirecting his attention to me. All I needed was a few moments of eye contact to lower his anxiety to a manageable level. Once I got some calm from him, I would offer a treat. Pretty quickly the presence of kids was neutralized. With treats at the ready, I told some kids that the dog was very shy and asked if they could help my friend Simon overcome his shyness. The kids agreed and I made sure to handle the dog as the little people fed him a treat. Unlike his owner, I didn't have a problem with Simon around kids, so the dog was a little less reactive. Simon clearly considered children a threat to him but may have also believed that his owner required his protection from them.

With me leading the introductions, Simon's tune changed over the course of an hour but I kept at it for a day before I passed him back to his owner. (By the way, it's amazing to see the caring concern of kids when they are doing something to help an animal. Even the boy who looked like he might scream, "Doggy!" and tackle Simon was suddenly gentle and focused.) Simon's sample size grew to the point where he understood that not all kids come equipped with sharp-nosed toy planes that seek the nearest eye. I use this example not only to highlight the importance of proper socialization but also to illustrate how teachable an adolescent dog can be.

CRITICAL MASS

In order to socialize a dog, it does not have to meet all of your Facebook friends, but it needs to meet plenty of people: friends, acquaintances, and strangers. It needs to meet strangers doing strange things—picking up the garbage, dropping off the mail—and it needs to contend with strangers who will be handling the dog: groomers, dog walkers, vets, friends, family, and possibly trainers.

You need to listen with your eyes in order to detect and prevent the development of phobias, fears, and foibles. In short, you need to speak a little dog. In no time, you two will be like a longtime married couple that can finish each other's sentences. The way you do this is by spending time with your dog and being social. Introduce your dog to people and other dogs, bring it to new places, and let your dog into your entire world (within reason).

For a dog to be fully socialized, it must be able to negotiate myriad environments, interactions, and objects, including but not limited to the following:

■ Locations: Home (inside and outside), other people's homes, crates, doghouses, dog parks, dog kennels, parks, bodies of water, veterinarians' offices, the groomer, etc.

■ People: Children, adults, the elderly, infants, handicapped people (wheelchairs, walkers—i.e., any and all who appear different will appear entirely different to a dog), people wearing big hats, sunglasses, carrying umbrellas; anything that alters appearance might make a dog think it's happened upon a new, potentially threatening species.

■ Animals: Your dog will also encounter other dogs, cats, rodents, as well as indigenous animals.

■ Objects: Furniture, different flooring surfaces (hardwood, waxed wood, carpeting, etc.), glass doors, toys and balls of all varieties, noisemaking objects, wood, paper, cardboard, Styrofoam, clothing, metal items; the list goes on to cars, buses, motorcycles, loud trucks (garbage trucks!), skateboards (a common issue), Rollerblades, bicycles, lawn mowers, washer/dryers, blenders, boats, vacuums, etc.

■ Sounds: Doorbells, singing, stereos, carts, fireworks, ice cream trucks, screaming, vehicles of all varieties, aircrafts—any and all of the above can create an aural alarm for a dog.

Dogs also have to be able to move through these environments and deal with things like garage doors, electric sliding doors, glass doors, stairwells, elevators, escalators, closing and opening doors, bathtubs, etc. Without needed guidance, this is a daunting proposition for a dog.

Dogs will need to be bathed, get their nails clipped, be flea-combed, be brushed (fur and teeth), be picked up by loved ones, and be accosted by overfriendly strangers. A veterinarian will take their temperature, look in their ears and mouth and between their toes, and do whatever else is needed at a checkup or in performing a basic procedure.

Dogs will need to deal with many of these sights, sounds, and experiences on their own. How many people are with their dog more often than not? Most dogs are going to gain their greatest experience solo, so be ready to discover what they've picked up on in their travels.

Let's get prepared. I am less of a proponent than many regarding the use of treats in teaching dogs the basic socialization techniques. I find they can be a distraction to the dog. Still, better safe than sorry, so keep some treats in your proverbial quiver, especially if working with a puppy. We'll begin with the first rule of etiquette: the dog introduction.

MEET AND GREET

Dogs need to meet people, as well as other dogs, and form positive associations. Let me say that again. Dogs need to meet people, as well as other dogs, and form positive associations. Meeting new people is easier, so let's start with meeting new dogs.

INTROS AND OUTROS

So, you're taking a Sunday stroll on a narrow sidewalk, and along comes a fellow human walking a strange dog. You nod in acknowledgment, and this person slows down, but the dog keeps going, straight in the path of your pooch. It is your job to make the introduction to this potential new canine friend. A well-socialized dog may know how to introduce itself, but we never know with whom our furry friend is coming into contact. Be first and never let the dog lead. In such instances, always keep your dog behind you.

■ Justin keeps Buster safely behind him as Erin approaches with a curious Chiquita. Justin is standing at an ideal angle. He can keep an eye on Buster while meeting the approaching dog.

■ Justin uses the hand signal to have Buster sit. Erin has also asked Chiquita to sit. They are at a very comfortable distance to begin a great introduction.

■ Justin makes sure that Buster is giving him his attention. Once confident that Buster is in a good place, he gives him the hand signal for "stay."

■ A Zen-like Buster exhibits masterful patience as Justin says hello to Chiquita. Note Justin's introductory gesture is to put his hand under the chin of Chiquita. Erin dutifully watches on.

■ Both dogs were so good about their intros that they're invited to say hello to each other. Note Justin's good monitoring position and the slack on the leash (sorry, Erin).

■ This is an example of what not to do. With the dogs in the lead the humans can't instruct and reactive behavior is a possibility. Why chance it?

Dogs do not relish the role of protector; rather, it makes them anxious, fearful, and aggressive.

When the dog goes first, problems can ensue. This is how leashes get tangled and dogs get riled. Things escalate in a hurry unless you lead and are in a position to remove your dog from the fray if necessary. In combustible situations, we all have the option of flight, fight, or freeze. When a dog is on a leash, flight is not an option, and in close proximity to another dog, freezing is not very viable, either. Fight is the only option. People who let their dog go first are now following their dog, which is precarious. This nonchalant approach often gives dogs the impression that they are the gatekeeper and protector, which appreciably ups the ante. Dogs do not relish the role of protector; rather, it makes them anxious, fearful, and aggressive. A dog in this position may think, "We've got incoming" every time it encounters another living thing around its owner.

Dogs react in many ways when they see one of their fellow brethren or sistren; excited, playful, fearful, aggressive, submissive, among the gamut of dog behaviors. They may crouch down, bark, or jump in playful or aggressive fashion, roll on their backs submissively, shake and cower in fear, or just stay cool as a cucumber. Irrespective of their reactions, it is our job to monitor the introduction.

- Create space. About ten feet away from the unfamiliar dog, ask your dog to sit. This teaches patience and halts any rambunctious behavior.

- Approach the new dog with your dog slightly behind you.

■ Be sure your dog is sitting as you reach out to allow the new dog to sniff your hand.

■ If your dog is calm and you like the new dog, invite your dog in.

■ Keep a close eye. If one dog plays too rough or goes under the hood to sniff with too much enthusiasm, the other dog may growl or snap to set a boundary. This is natural and no need to be alarmed. Some dogs need to learn the manners of sniffing. Although they may mean well, even well-behaved dogs will go on high alert or simply react when another dog gets up in their grill, so to speak. Any mild escalation can usually be dealt with by separating your dog and having him sit for a few moments. Such time-outs give dogs a chance to learn proper introductions and play. However, if either dog appears stiff in posture, excitable, or heads in for a face-to-face, use your leash to create space. In urgent situations, step in with your knee to create space.

In general, people are horrendous at dog introductions. They may ask if your dog is friendly, and, before you've even answered, their dog can be all over yours. Practice good etiquette by always being first so everyone can be comfortable. When a dog goes eye-to-eye with another dog, it can be a challenge. In this rare circumstance, use your leash to pull back and your knee to intercede between the dogs. Risking a bite on a bent knee is small potatoes compared to breaking up two dogs locked on each other.

People with friendly dogs often drop their leashes whenever their dog is sniffing another. They may appear to be off to a good start, but tensions can escalate, especially when only one dog is on leash. Be extremely mindful in monitoring.

NICE PEOPLE

For a dog that is shy or nervous with people, treats can actually go a long way. That said, they are not to be used in making dog introductions as problems can arise. The combination of treats and being petted is a potent way to form positive associations. Save for the treats, the principles in meeting strangers are the same as in meeting other dogs.

- The key is to be first. Your dog will sense that it is safe.

For a couple of months:

- Ask new people to introduce themselves with a treat.

- Practice this technique on and off the leash.

- Practice this inside and outside your home.

The goal is to socialize and expose your dog to a wide variety of people, places, and things. This is how dogs develop confidence and a sense of security. A dog that is wary of people, and even a dog that acts out aggressively, is generally lacking confidence, which can be traced to unfamiliarity. Let your dog meet people of all sizes, races, creeds, and kinds. I mean that. Fear of the unknown can wreak havoc, so please observe your dog in order to be a good chaperone.

■ Dog Greeting 1—The wrong way: Mara is literally over the top on this one. When meeting a dog, putting one's head over their body can feel invasive and reaching one's hand over their head to pet them can also alarm a dog.

■ Dog Greeting 2—The correct way: Dave turns sideways and makes his big self smaller. He also offers his hand for Pacino to sniff. This shows good manners and can put an apprehensive dog at ease.

■ Dog Greeting 3—Dave's hands go under Pacino's chin as he happily accepts Dave's warm greetings.

By listening with your eyes, you will uncover the situations that your dog is particularly reactive to and then be able to focus on these "triggers."

- Triggers need to be addressed, not avoided.

- Limiting a dog's exposure to triggers exacerbates the behavior. Just ask Simon.

BABY STEPS

Exposure therapy is a technique used by mental health professionals to treat people with phobias, fears, and some obsessive-compulsive behaviors. In this straightforward form of treatment, the client is slowly exposed to the source of his trouble and, little by little, the fear diminishes. Integrating your dog fully into your life is a preventative form of exposure therapy. For dogs that have triggers, exposure therapy is essential. It must be practiced very gradually. One can go too fast but not too slow. In the case of acute aggression or problems in the extreme, it is wise to speak with a professional first.

TRIPPING THE TRIGGER

The mailman is the archetypal trigger person for dogs. Fortunately, the fix can be easy. Should your dog terrorize the mail carrier, kindly ask her to feed your dog a treat or throw a ball and let the healing begin. Dogs can be redirected to form new associations, and redirection holds the key.

■ Chiquita has been alerted to something and has run ahead, desperately wanting to check it out. A concerned Justin weighs the situation.

■ Justin does not like Chiquita's energy and immediately redirects her to head in the opposite direction of the stimulus.

■ Justin shuffles backward, calling Chiquita in a happy tone that motivates her to pay more attention to him rather than the triggering stimulus.

■ Justin keeps Chiquita's attention by having her engage in the "sit" command.

■ He continues to redirect her impulsive desires onto something more productive by having her perform the "down" command.

■ Chiquita receives due praise for performing her commands so well in the face of urgent distraction. At this juncture, a calmer Chiquita can effectively navigate the road ahead.

The concept of redirection could go anywhere in the book, as it applies to all facets of dog husbandry, but I chose socialization because it is so clearly helpful in adjusting and molding how a dog interacts with the world.

The term "redirection" is often used in the case of dog aggression. When a dog is attacking another animal and someone tries to break it up, the dog may end up biting that person without realizing. It will be said that the dog redirected. The term is also used to mean transferring a negatively reacting dog's attention onto a preferred alternative. A dog barking incessantly at the approaching mailman can be lured with a reward, directed to a destination spot, and taught to sit when the mailman arrives. I lure the dog with the promise of a treat but give the dog a choice, just like I did with Maya. In this case, the question would be: "Would you prefer to bark your lungs out, or would you like to play a game called 'The Mailman's Here'?" In this game, the dog gets to go to a spot, have a seat, and be rewarded and praised by a happy owner. Should it be a double-jackpot day, the dog can be introduced to the mailman and get yet another reward.

The actual redirection occurs just before the dog's knee-jerk reaction. The moment the ears go up (because the mailman is coming) is the moment the game begins.

Even in relatively extreme cases, redirection can work wonders. It can even help with aggression issues. Dogs that appear to be aggressive are generally fearful, so they will let out a warning growl. A growl is something to take seriously enough but it's usually a dog communicating discomfort with a given situation. Removing your dog from the situation is the first move if aggression is a possibility. In more innocuous scenarios, such as a whirring vacuum cleaner, try redirecting the dog's attention to a reward. This simple method can be especially helpful with skateboards, loud trucks, and alarming noises in general. A dog that is fearful of a particular person should be kept at a safe distance while that person remains in sight.

My Chiquita was fearful of men in hats, particularly at night. Strange but true. When a man wearing any type of hat would walk by, she would lower her head and pin on them before breaking into a growl. To treat this issue, I began by exposing her to some fedora wearers (not hard to find) from a distance where she was concerned, but not reactive.

Right at the first tell—when she lowered her head—I'd say her name with excitement. When she looked at me, I'd show her a treat but would not give it to her. I did not want her to associate the reward as praise for lowering her head in fear. Instead, I'd playfully shuffle backward a few steps, call her to me, ask her to sit, and then lie down before giving her the reward. As her attention became divided, she calmed some and was able to sense that I did not consider the fedora-wearing passerby a threat. I didn't tell her that men under age sixty wearing fedoras get on my nerves. My positive attitude helped considerably, so my next move was to ask a hat-wearing stranger to walk by Chiquita and me. One guy was nice enough to walk by a few times, getting closer and closer with each pass. This is an example of exposure and proximity training. Chiquita had gotten largely over the issue from a distance, so the proximity piece moved quickly.

THE RIGHT TOUCH

Thus far we've addressed introductions, the importance of having your dog meet all types of people, and the concept of redirection in cases where a dog has triggers that cause unpleasant reactions. Now we have to consider something that any creature in the animal kingdom would be uncomfortable with, without some practice.

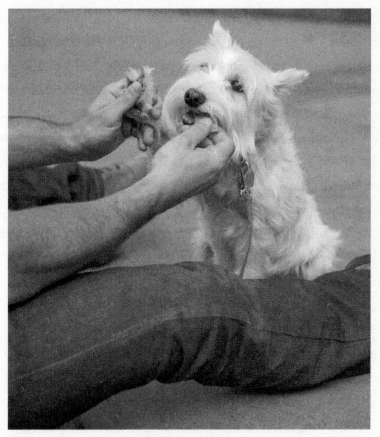

■ Justin uses treats and inspects Kennedy's paw. By making positive associations with being handled, Kennedy will be far happier visiting the vet and groomer.

All dogs need to get used to being handled. Dogs will be groomed, have their teeth brushed, visit the veterinarian for an examination, and perhaps have to deal with a child tugging its leg or pulling its tail. This is not something dogs are automatically prepared for (to this day, I hate when people pull my tail).

To form sound associations with being handled, a dog must be touched, mushed, petted, and basically massaged everywhere. This includes some sensitive places like its mouth, ears, paws, gums, and teeth. For a dog to be vet-friendly and childproof, the best thing to do is start having those closest to the dog handle them. Give him a lengthy petting, beginning with the foolproof belly rub, before you move on to more sensitive areas. Should a dog doth protest too much, go back to the belly or a favorite spot and begin again. Treats will again come in handy as a dog catches on quickly to the fact that being petted and fed simultaneously is nothing short of awesome. Have others do the same, and with practice, even a touchy dog can be lulled and persuaded into being examined. This technique is also helpful in getting dogs to submit to dreaded activities like teeth brushing and nail clipping.

MAKING FRIENDS

Having someone who can keep an eye on your pooch and provide a playdate is invaluable. Dogs need to be around other dogs and people on a regular basis. In some areas, this can be challenging, but for the most part, there are local dog parks and fellow dog owners close by.

Dogs unfortunately do not get along with every dog; nor should they be expected to. I don't expect a dog to happily interact with every other dog at the local dog run. A well-balanced dog can find friends but also play on its own, even in a park full of fellow canines.

MY DOG IS TROUBLE

This specifically refers to dogs that have shown signs of aggression toward other dogs or been in a fight and have subsequently become more aggressive. I will address general aggression in Chapter 9, "Living in the Solution," under the heading Aggression/Territorial Behavior.

People are rightly concerned if their dog has been in an altercation before. It is nothing short of scary to see dogs going medieval on one another. While a fight can affect a dog, people tend to take it much harder. I've seen so many dogs that are poorly socialized because, at one point or another, they got into a fight, and their owners have since kept them relatively isolated. It is difficult to get good information on this subject, as aggression is a scenario that no one wants to tackle sight unseen. While I agree, I can say that if your dog got off to a bad start with a neighbor's dog or got into it at the dog run, there is hope.

Dogs that are unpredictably aggressive with other dogs, or dogs that have become aggressive since being in a fight, need lengthier introductions. Gradual exposure is the ticket, with the emphasis on "gradual." Cooperation from fellow dog owners is required, so don't be too proud to beg, borrow, or bribe a willing dog owner.

Begin by using a short lead; no more than six feet in length and ideally four. Make sure the leash is super secure in your hand but not taut (we do not want to communicate tension).

- With both dogs on leash, calmly say hello from roughly twenty feet.

- Slowly move closer but stay at a distance where the dogs are not reactive.

- Use a treat to redirect the dog should it begin to act up.

- Also use your leash to redirect—remain calm so you don't put unnecessary pressure on the lead as you break your dog's fixation on the other dog.

- Look for stress clues, such as hackling (in which the hairs on the neck are raised) or pinning (fixating on the other dog or stiffness in the body).

- At any sign of stress, get more space.

- When the dog is calm, very slowly make your way over to your friend.

- Keep dogs separated by both owners—two humans apart.

- With the leash short but not taut, shake hands with your fellow human while continuing to keep the dogs at a distance.

- With the dogs on the outside of both parties, walk together and make sure the dogs aren't glowering at each other.

It is up to the owners not to stress the dogs by holding the leash too tightly. A short leash can still have slack. After ten minutes of walking together, the dogs should be close to accustomed to each other's presence.

Signs to look for:

- The dog's looking away or sniffing objects.

- The dog attempts to engage its owner.

- The dog appears interested in something besides the other dog.

- If you come to a stop, the dog sits.

- Any sign that communicates disinterest or lack of concern.

Go slow, be patient, and when you're confident, allow the dogs to sniff each other from the back and then separate them once more. Dogs will rarely attack from the back. Let them trail each other by a few feet. When you are comfortable, use the steps described in "Intros and Outros" to let the dogs briefly into each other's space (but not nose to nose), and build up the time until they can freely socialize. Should an aggressive dog have to meet another dog indoors, keep both dogs on leash and monitor closely. Enclosed spaces can heighten tensions. To fight-proof the environment, keep toys, chew sticks, food, and food bowls away because spats over play objects or food are not uncommon. Once the dog is getting on better with others of his kind, an abbreviated version of this ritual can be performed.

NIPPING/MOUTHING

Mouthing is natural for dogs, as a dog's mouth acts as its hands. Mother dogs use the same jaws to pick up their puppies as they do to hunt prey, while dogs at play mouth each other around the scruff of the neck and playfully nip at each other's limbs. It is through this social play that dogs, especially puppies, learn bite inhibition and appropriate bite pressure. A dog will yelp when bitten too hard, at which time the other dog should back off. Puppies don't know the difference between mouthing canines or humans until we show them.

Observe the difference between play mouthing and true aggression. Families with young children and puppies become alarmed that the dog is aggressive when mouthing and nipping occur.

It is an absolute must that dogs learn bite pressure through socialization. Fellow dogs will do a far better job teaching appropriate bite pressure, as this is an instinctive need. Socializing with other dogs will do wonders to limit a young dog's need to mouth/nip on humans.

The most common mistake is the overcorrection of this instinctual behavior. While corrections in general are to be used sparingly, a mouthing dog is in an excited state, so any type of reactive reprimanding will not help the issue. Worse yet, such histrionics will engender defensive behavior, which can come in the form of biting as play mouthing turns to aggression.

To teach bite inhibition, one can allow gentle mouthing of the skin or not permit any skin contact whatsoever. This is a personal choice.

▪ Let your dog mouth toys or tug items as you hold them.

▪ When the dog makes contact with your skin, an "ehh-ehh!" or "ouch!," followed by turning away from the dog for five to ten seconds, is a time-honored technique. The dog will figure out that humans have pretty fragile skin and don't appreciate when their pup practices mouthing on them.

▪ Resume play. If the dog is not getting it, give a big "ouch!" and stand up.

▪ Walk out of the room in a huff: The dog can sense that someone isn't happy and that play may be in jeopardy. Wait five minutes and go back.

▪ Use the "gentle mouth," "leave it," and "drop it" commands. These are all excellent commands that can help with impulse control.

▪ Redirect mouthing of the inappropriate object or people onto chew items.

▪ Dog mouths a wrist or hand: say, "ehh-ehh!" and introduce the tug toy instead.

It may seem counterintuitive to introduce a chew toy to an animal with a mouthing problem, but it is a constructive outlet for the behavior. Be sure to keep the chew toys in rotation so they remain novel and, for an added attraction, soak a rope toy or rubber bone in chicken stock.

BETTER TO GIVE

There is no redeeming value in having a dog that is ornery and on edge or fearful and submissive. The dog is certainly not having any fun. When our relationship with dogs got under way, there were a lot less people on the planet. Their roles were very different and given their genetic makeup, a lot easier to fill. Meeting these difficulties should be part of the continuing process that is socialization for both man and dog.

I would have to say the most enduring role that we still share with dogs is our desire for affection from each other. Studies have shown that petting a dog lowers levels of epinephrine and norepinephrine (relaxes and reduces anxiety and depression), lowers blood pressure, increases endorphins as well as oxytocin levels (oxytocin is known as the "love hormone"). I can't sell being affectionate toward your dog better than that.

Socialize your dog so it may healthily interact with friends and strangers alike, and teach the dog that it is safe to be handled by health care professionals and groomers. A little affection goes a long way. Take dogs to the usual places, and let them venture with you into more challenging environments so they may gain needed confidence and security.

CHAPTER 9

LIVING IN THE SOLUTION

"If there are no dogs in Heaven,
then when I die I want to go where they went."
—WILL ROGERS

You've been such good sports by taking on all this responsibility and learning technical jargon, it's time to offer a "gimme." The following is a list of common canine problems and solutions. It is impossible to address every permutation of a problem and its potential causes, so being observant is always part of the fix. You will need to have a handle on the following:

Desensitization
As you recall from socialization, a dog's inability to control its reactions to people, animals, objects, places, and sounds is a fairly common problem that can result in:

- Aggressive behaviors—barking and lunging to attack.

- Fearful behaviors—trembling, urinating, fleeing, hiding, or shutting down.

- Other behaviors may include panting, whining, howling, and spinning.

To treat these, we incrementally expose the dog to the triggering stimulus in a nonthreatening way. With time and practice, a neutral to positive response can be formed.

Redirection

Always have something at the ready to grab the dog's attention as it begins to react. That may be a reward or in acute conditions even a negative reinforcer, such as a spray from a water bottle. The idea is to "snap" the dog out of the dangerous mode it is threatening to go into.

Compassionate Corrections

Always guide the dog to a reward or a more relaxed state. Even the aforementioned spray from a water bottle, while not pleasant, can serve to distract a dog from going into flight or fight.

Leash Pressure

The leash is a way we communicate with dogs. A well-trained dog and skilled handler "talk" to each other through the leash. Developing leash skills takes nothing but attentive practice. Any pull should be subtle and short, but never yank or snap the leash. To cue the dog, it is most effective to pull upward and less is always more. Think of it as a tap on the shoulder. A subtle tap will get someone's attention just as well as a smack. Should yanking feel necessary to restrain a dog in dealing with common occurrences and situations, desensitization and handling work is required.

Tools

A tension gate (similar to a baby gate) or a crate in the home is helpful for desensitizing a dog, because either one separates the dog from the triggering stimulus. Other tools should include treats, shorter leads (four-foot nylon leashes), chew toys, tug toys, and in some cases, longer training leashes (fifteen to thirty feet), as well as head halter collars.

HOME REACTIVITY

Home reactivity refers to dogs triggered by children, other animals, or even objects like vacuum cleaners inside the home. By "reactivity," I do not necessarily mean aggression but barking, skittish behavior, and hyper concern all constitute reactivity. To properly limit the risk and reactivity, a tension gate is very helpful to allow a dog to be safely exposed to its perceived nemesis.

Put the dog behind a gate to sequester it from the trigger, but keep the trigger close enough so the dog is aware of the upsetting presence. Offer a toy or chew stick to play with and reward calm behavior. Once there is an established level of calm from the dog, remove the gate and use the down/stay command with the dog on a leash. Be careful of any flare-ups, and closely monitor the interaction between the dog and the stimulus—i.e., the other dog, child, or object. Once the dog is nonreactive, welcome him to sit or lie closer to the stimulus but first make sure he is not fixating on the trigger. Slowly (on leash) allow the dog to investigate by politely sniffing the object, person, or animal while being closely watched.

■ Using the gate to create separation while offering line of sight, all parties acclimate to each other's presence. Justin rewards Pacino for calm behavior.

■ Pacino was so calm that Justin removed the gate, but keeps him on the leash, sitting in a destination spot (the mat).

■ Justin monitors and physically remains between the dog and the potentially triggering or triggered stimulus, aka Matthew.

■ Justin detects the calm being exhibited by everyone, so he moves the mat closer to Matthew while maintaining his position between Pacino and the little man.

■ Pacino has been so well behaved, Justin (still monitoring) has asked Matthew's mom to give him a treat.

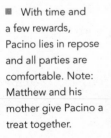

■ With time and a few rewards, Pacino lies in repose and all parties are comfortable. Note: Matthew and his mother give Pacino a treat together.

PULLING/HALTING ON LEASH

Dogs pull for many understandable reasons: They are faster than people, they engage the world more enthusiastically than we do, and they have their own agenda as to where they wish to go. The number one reason dogs pull is because it works, and fixing this is a matter of not permitting it. For a dog that is a particularly tough walk, get a hold of a head halter collar to go with your four-foot leash.

Head Halter Collars

The head halter is an excellent tool for pullers, reactive dogs, and hyper dogs. It goes around the dog's head and over the nose. It is similar to a horse's halter. It attaches to the leash from just under the dog's chin and allows the handler to lead the dog from the cockpit (its nose). Some people irrationally balk at using halter collars because they mistake them for muzzles, which are used on aggressive dogs. Although the halter attaches to the dog's muzzle it is *not* a muzzle, as dogs can open their mouths, which allows them to consume treats and play with tug toys or balls (also recommended to ease the transition). Dogs will often rub and paw at the halter to get it off their face. It is an adjustment not dissimilar to that of a child who resists wearing a retainer. Start by using the halter for short periods and keep the pace brisk, as dogs are less prone to fuss with the halter when moving at a faster clip.

Warning

Once a dog gets into pawing at the halter, it can become an obsession. Should the dog paw at the collar, give the leash a gentle shake. Issue a warning like "ehh-ehh," and redirect him to a toy or treat, or begin to jog so he acclimates. This adjustment can take anywhere from a few hours to a few weeks.

Pulling/Lunging

The first thing to do with a pulling dog is to stop in your tracks and wait. Give the dog time to figure out that pulling is getting him nowhere. This may have to be repeated any number of times before he catches on. I'd guesstimate that this number is roughly equivalent to the amount of times the pulling was successful.

Slow the Walk

Some dogs begin by subtly pulling and inching ahead or slowly changing direction. A little leash pressure and course correction helps, but simply slowing down, not giving in, and letting the dog fall in line is more effective.

The Active Walk

The active walk combines walking and the use of the heeling technique, as described in Chapter 7, "Command Central." This helps the dog's concentration, offers him some treats to work for, and slowly lets him know that you are leading. With time, the dog will recognize that his job is to be a good partner by walking calmly alongside you. It is also a great way to work some training into a walk.

Check Yourself

Frustration sets in pretty quickly in dealing with a pulling dog. Tension can quickly manifest, and before you know it, the walker is unwittingly exerting excessive leash pressure. That leash is a lightning rod, so give calm to get calm, and allow the leash some slack.

Prevent Defense

Do not leash up an excited dog and expect a calm walk. Encourage a calm mind state by having the dog sit as the leash is put on. It's good practice to have the dog stay for a moment before heading out the door.

HALTING

Halting is the opposite of pulling. This is when a dog puts the brakes on and refuses to walk. It is very common in puppies and dogs that lack confidence.

Motivating Movement

Toys, treats, enthusiasm, and the company of other dogs can be just the ticket. Once the dog is moving, look for signs that the halting is coming. Dogs tend to fall into routines as they go into halt or even shutdown (remember Harry the bulldog?). Identifying the signs enables one to pull the dog through the funk by breaking into a trot or run. Always continue to motivate a dog with an enthusiasm that says, "Hey, we're having fun." An upbeat attitude can keep the dog from getting stuck in the quicksand. You might also try walking at a faster clip or jogging.

Stay Strong

Do not falter when that meditative two-hour walk just isn't happening. Start with short walks to build time and confidence. Take more walks, which can be as short as a trip to the mailbox. Short walks help to build confidence for longer walks, and the more the dog is on leash with you, the more it will catch on to the joys of walking.

I used to take my friend's uneasy dog to a deli where the owner would give him a bite of roast beef and I would mark it with the word "deli." After a week, if I grabbed the leash and said, "Deli," the dog would all but bound there. Bring treats.

Danger Zones

Temporarily stay away from "bad places." Should a dog freeze up in a specific place, he has associated this spot with halting. Pick him up and take him a few dozen yards away and begin walking. Once some progress has been made, return to the scene of the crime and move him through.

GARBAGE MOUTH

Eating feces (coprophagy) may be disgusting to us, but it's natural for some dogs. And a chicken bone on the sidewalk? No one can blame them. Some dogs just can't say no to anything that has a smell and fits in their mouth.

Prevent Defense

Check with a veterinarian to make sure the dog's diet is providing the sufficient nutrients, as a deficiency can occasionally be the cause. Many dogs will eat their own feces around the backyard or at a dog park. Monitor this behavior and do your best to keep the area devoid of fecal matter, because a dog can't eat what's not there. Redirect with the "leave it" command. When your dog encounters an edible that is not "kosher," say, "Leave it," walk the dog away from temptation, and then reward.

I trained a dog that ate goose excrement near a pond where she was able to run freely off leash. The first thing I did was to teach the "leave it" command, keeping the dog on a twenty-foot training leash. The next step was to have the owner keep the dog away from the pond for two weeks. After the two weeks were up, they returned to the pond, where the owner monitored the dog for any attempts at unwanted eating. After a few visits, the behavior ceased.

BARKING AT THE DOORBELL AND COMPANY

The number one perpetuator of this behavior is the dog owner who barks back at the dog. "Shush! Stop it! Stop barking! Knock it off!" delivered at decibel levels louder than the dog's is not a deterrent. The message to the dog is: "When the bell rings, we all begin to bark." Other culprits are inadequate socialization, insufficient exercise, and no understanding of the "down" or "stay" command.

The Doorbell Game

It is not bad for a dog to bark and effectively say, "Hey, someone's here," when the doorbell rings. Excessive barking and carrying on is another thing. The protocol should be to thank the dog for alerting you that there is a guest at the door. The dog should then be led to a designated spot and be able to wait while the guest is greeted. Once the guest is inside, the four-legged family member should be called over to say hello.

- Use the "go to spot" command followed by "stay."

- The destination spot should be a few yards from the front door and provide an unobstructed line of sight for the dog.

- The spot should be something the dog likes to sit on that is accessible. Do not use anything that requires climbing into.

Desensitization

Use the "go to spot" command followed by "stay" and have someone ring the doorbell. Moderate barking in response to the ring is fine so long as the dog stays in the designated spot. Reward the dog for staying and being less reactive to the sound.

How to Play the Game

Instruct the dog to stay in the designated place. At first, use the leash to bring the dog back to the spot if he moves off it. Holding eye contact with the dog, walk backward toward the door, return, and reward. Repeat, but this time knock on your own door and/or ring the bell yourself before returning and rewarding. As progress is

■ Justin has Pacino sit on a soft mat that offers full line of sight to the door. The mat/bed is minimal so it's easy on and off for Pacino.

■ Justin gives him the hand signal for "stay." Note: Justin's hand position makes it impossible for Pacino to miss his cue.

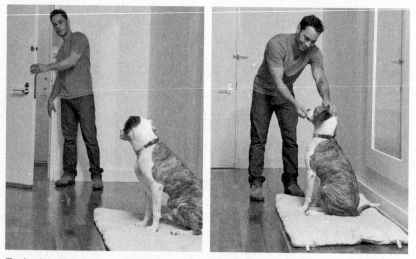

■ Justin maintains eye contact as he opens the door. He will then proceed to knock on the door to simulate sounds Pacino will associate with arriving guests. Let's hope Pacino stays put.

■ Justin returns to Pacino and rewards him for staying on the mat for the whole exercise.

■ With Pacino off doing his own thing, Justin surprises him by ringing the doorbell.

■ Pacino's barks, running to the door as if to say, "There's someone at the door! This is the best thing ever!"

■ Justin lures Pacino with the promise of a treat with one contingency: Pacino must contain his enthusiasm and wait patiently on his mat.

made, eye contact won't be necessary and you can try allowing other people to ring the bell. To raise the stakes, ring the doorbell multiple times and swing the door open. When the dog stays, reward and repeat. Should the dog still be struggling, do it quietly and retain eye contact. As a final exam, have a short conversation with an invisible person outside the door. Reward the dog for positive behavior.

Once the dog is desensitized to the sound of the doorbell and can stay in his spot, we move to a real-world rehearsal by turning the dog loose. While he is freely roaming the house, ring the doorbell and signal your dog to go to the spot, or happily take him there if he's still learning. The dog may bark to say, "Hey! Someone's here!" to which you reply, "Thanks," and show the dog the reward. Give the dog a moment to calm down and issue a "stay" before going to the door. Open the door, have a real or imaginary conversation, close the door, return, and reward. Have everyone who lives in the house ring the doorbell when they come home.

Once eighty percent success has been achieved, practice the entire ritual and delay the reward until the end of the exercise.

Warning

Maintain realistic expectations by asking guests to avoid loud, excited greetings of the dog. Sessions should be short and upbeat.

Cheat

Keep the dog on a leash and use the "sit" command as company enters the home.

■ Practice makes real-life scenarios go smoothly. After following the rehearsed steps, Justin opens the door and greets Rochelle as Pacino does him proud by staying on the mat.

■ Justin invites Pacino up for a little introduction and uses his leash to guide him.

■ Pacino outdoes Justin by offering his paw to greet Rochelle.

HYPERACTIVITY

Symptoms

Jumping on people, constant attention seeking, pushy behavior, rough play, pestering for affection, as well as excessive nipping, mouthing, barking, whimpering, etc. Not hard to identify.

Warning

Dogs may be extra-prone to behaving this way around kids. At times, kids' voices and demonstrative gestures heat up the play response, which keeps dogs in excited states.

Culprits

Inadequate exercise, a dog too isolated from people and other dogs, and a lack of structured activities.

Prevention

The first line of defense is structured exercise. Exercise the dog adequately with jogging, fetch, tug-of-war, and any activity where agility can come into play. Do not roughhouse with the dog. Even when a dog is by itself, monitor energy levels and do your best to avoid a ramp-up. Simply keeping your dog company can do wonders for bringing down energy levels and preventing them from spiking in the first place. Always exercise the dog before guests arrives.

Commands

"Down" and "stay" are the biggies. After exercise, give the dog a few minutes to unwind. Bring him to his bed or place of rest and have him stay. Expect whining or barking, but don't give in; a dog needs to learn to process anxious feelings in order to settle down.

Gate/Crate

When "down/stay" isn't doing the trick, gating or crating a dog can help it unwind. Use proper judgment in finding a calm place.

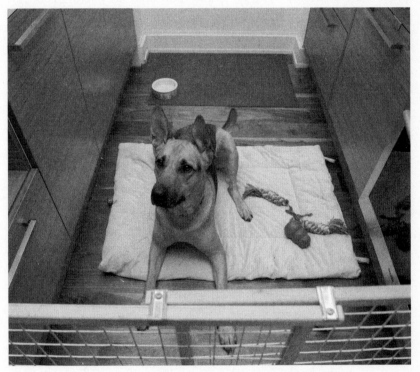

■ Shamon is gated in a dog-proofed area. He has water, a bed, stainless-steel appliances, some toys, and a peanut butter–filled rubber treat to work on.

The Turn-away

Some dogs get the message to calm down if you simply turn your back and ignore them. Turn away, and give the dog a minute to settle down.

Leash on in the House

Keeping a leash on the dog in the house prevents it from jumping on people and pestering. "No," "off," and "ehh-ehh" are useful in concert with using the leash to stop unwanted behaviors. Use "sit" to guide the dog to a reward. Keeping a leash on when company is present is not a bad idea for some dogs.

Warning

Hyperactive dogs are typically difficult to discourage, so keep your cool. Never keep a leash on a dog that is not being monitored, as leashes can get snagged and dogs can choke themselves.

When I have guests over, my dogs get excited. I allow them to greet friends, and I ask my friends not to wind them up. I put the dogs in a down/stay and give them each a frozen rubber toy that holds peanut butter so they will be occupied while we suffer through a Giants game, for example. By the time they finish the treat, they are calm and acclimated to the company. From there, they can do as they please. They may interact with my friends, but at this point, they are perfectly well behaved.

BEGGING/WHINING

Do not feed a dog when it begs. Ignore begging and whining, and the dog will realize they do not work.

Prevention
Having a dog earn a meal via training can be vital. When preparing food, use "sit" and "stay" to keep the dog out of the kitchen and at a manageable distance. Always have your dog sit before feeding, and hold the food bowl for a three-count before placing it on the floor.

■ With Rochelle in the captain's chair, the irreverent Gustav sits on leash as Dave and Justin enjoy dessert. From this position, Rochelle can effectively keep an eye on Gustav.

When you're eating, use the "sit" and "stay" commands in a designated spot so the dog makes the association as to where it is supposed to be while people are eating. Don't forget to reward the dog; you may be getting up and rewarding every few minutes at first. With each passing meal, extend the time between rewards until you can sit through an entire meal uninterrupted.

Cheat
Give the dog a treat that takes some time to consume. Freezing the previously mentioned rubber toy filled with peanut butter makes the treat last. Have the dog consume the treat in a crate or behind a gate during meals.

HOUSE TRAINING

Time and Space
Timing is key. Know when the dog's bladder is full and have him in the appropriate place when he is ready to relieve himself. (Thank you, Professor Obvious.)

In or Out
When dogs are young, elderly, disabled, sick, or confined to an apartment that offers no outdoor outlet, pee pads may be necessary. For healthy dogs, pee pads give the message that it's acceptable for a dog to relieve itself indoors so I'd advise against them.

Rules

Never scold a dog for going in the house, under any circumstance, or the dog will look for remote areas of the home to do its business. Punishing an animal for going to the bathroom is abusive.

Observe

There's that word again. After the dog is done eating and drinking, figure out roughly how long it takes until he needs to go, then take him outside.

Tips

When you are not at home, a dog should have its own place, like a crate or gated area. It won't compromise the integrity of its space unless forced to. Upon returning, take the dog outside immediately to relieve itself.

Prevention

No unattended play indoors, since excited dogs are more prone to relieve themselves.

Consistency

When using pads, keep them in the same place so an association gets formed with a particular spot. For puppies, close to the front door works, since they're one step away from the great outdoors.

Shaping

If the dog makes an effort to hit the target but misses, the effort is still worthy of a reward.

Scenting

Keeping a little urine on the pad or taking the dog to the same spot outside is a way the dog can identify this as the place to go.

Off-target

Keep dogs away from areas and furniture where unwanted marking is occurring. If there is a certain spot on the rug, roll it up or keep the dog out of that room until properly house trained.

Other Culprits

Urinary tract infections, dietary changes, separation anxiety, excitement, or submissive urination can impede progress.

FOOD AGGRESSION/RESOURCE GUARDING

Warning

For anything other than minor issues, please see a professional. It's natural for dogs to be protective around toys and food, so food aggression/resource guarding can be a difficult issue.

Desensitization

It does a world of good to regularly hand-feed your dog, have the dog earn its meals via training, and put treats into the dog's bowl while it is eating. Practice the "leave it" and "drop it" command with chews and toys so it becomes accustomed to relinquishing things upon your request.

Respect the Dog's Boundaries

Less is more in this case. Make only necessary contact while the dog is eating. You should not be afraid to approach your dog, either. My rule is a dog should be no more tolerant than a person would be if someone were to pet her while she ate: I don't expect the dog to like it, but aggression is unacceptable.

While the dog is eating, stand a few yards away and say, "Hi, puppy!" before tossing a few treats. Repeat this every ten to fifteen seconds until the meal is finished. Perform this with each and every meal until there are no signs of guarding or aggression. It may take anywhere from a week to a couple of months, so patience is a needed virtue.

With time, move closer to the bowl when you drop the treats. Monitor tension levels and keep pushing the boundary, so long as it doesn't elicit any aggressive or defensive responses. In approaching a highly reactive dog, it is wise to remain on the opposite side of a gate or tether the dog.

Once you can stand next to the dog's bowl while the dog is eating, greet her and offer a treat from your hand or a lick of peanut butter off a spoon and then walk away. Return and repeat until the meal is finished. When the dog is comfortable with this, stand next to her, say, "Hiya, puppy," and gently touch her back. As the dog looks up, offer a treat.

After she's eaten, have her walk a few feet away from her food bowl and sit. Pick up and handle her food bowl as she watches. Place a treat in the bowl and have her consume the treat while you hold the bowl. From there, place another treat in the bowl and put the bowl on the floor in front of the dog. When she finishes, say, "Good dog," have her sit, pick up the bowl, and place another treat in it. Perform enough repetitions to feel comfortable before moving on. Finally, while the dog is eating some mundane dry food, place a more exciting food (such as a piece of chicken) in the bowl. Once you're able to contend with the above scenarios, guard against relapses by periodically touching your dog and dropping a treat while the dog is eating.

Anxieties/Compulsions/Obsessions

Excessive and strange behavior patterns can surface for no apparent reason. These behaviors run the gamut from odd to comical to exhausting, disturbing, and harmful. A few common ones follow. If your particular issue isn't on the list, pretend that it is by identifying with the family of behavior. When I first got my dogs, I was easily convinced that any hiccup was unique to my dog. Dog anxieties, compulsions, and obsessions fall into categories of behavior and standard treatments do apply.

Signs

Excessive barking, licking or chewing of self or objects, biting at the air, chasing tail or spinning, whining, scratching of self or objects, chasing, staring or barking at objects, shadows, reflections, digging on hard surfaces (floors), fixating on objects, destruction of household items, marking, pacing, and thousands of others.

Warning

The first thing is to visit the vet to rule out medical problems. Do not punish or scold a dog for compulsive or obsessive behaviors, as it is likely already stressed. Do not coddle or baby the dog when it acts out.

Culprits

Inadequate exercise, boredom, lack of socialization and structure.

Treatment

The first treatment is always increased exercise with the owners. Long walks replete with commands, playing games, and the general redirection of anxious energies onto exercise are the first steps. In many cases, the pattern is a script being followed, so breaking the routine is essential. Additional socialization is also typically needed. Trips to the dog park will help and setting up playdates with other dogs can thwart the onset of these "cabin fever"–type symptoms.

Keep your dog company and try to catch it as it enters into its compulsive script. The dog may offer a window where redirection can occur. For example, a dog that licks compulsively will often stare at the target body part before commencement. It is possible to redirect the dog's attention onto something like a loud squeaking toy and lure it into some fetch. Enormous patience can be required here; once the dog goes into the "zone," it can take a while to unwind.

I once worked with a Westie named Molly who would bark uncontrollably at reflections being cast on the kitchen ceiling. Her bowl was made of stainless steel, and whenever there was light in the kitchen, it would reflect off the bowl onto the ceiling. Using a matte plastic bowl did not do the trick, because there were always reflections from incoming light. I took Molly just outside the kitchen and had her sit/stay before introducing her favorite ball. With Molly watching from just beyond the kitchen, I held her bowl in my hands and used it to create a momentary reflection off the ceiling. Before she could react, the reflection was gone, but she still wanted to engage the compulsion. She was torn between the reflection and her desire to play ball with me. After creating a few more reflections, she was far less reactive and finally, she sat quietly. As a reward, I tossed the ball into the living room and played with her some. I continued to make the reflections last longer, and would only toss the ball when she was non-reactive. Finally, we found our way into the kitchen and practiced some more. Within an hour, she was good. Molly's owner continued to practice with her for about a week before the reaction was entirely gone.

SEPARATION ANXIETY

Separation anxiety is as it sounds—a condition where dogs have difficulty being separated from their owner. Very often, these dogs react stressfully to the departure of anyone they know. In minor cases, it can be endearing. A dog we work with named Gustav (pictured on page 209) appears to have separation anxiety from people he just met. He'll pull on the leash and watch near strangers walk away as if he knows they're headed off on some fateful voyage. What makes this okay is that once the person is out of sight, Gustav transitions very quickly from his state of longing to his usual "what are we doing now, right now, this moment is everything" disposition. When dogs do not make this transition, they often go into states of panic and stay there. Please make sure to find your way down to "Jealous Behavior," as the two very often go hand in hand.

Warning

For severe issues, please consult a professional.

Culprits

Previous abandonment, spoiling, insufficient exercise, lack of socialization, no "job."

When a dog sees a door closing behind a person, it has no knowledge that the person is ever coming back. The moment someone is out of view and scent range, to the dog, that person is potentially gone forever. Considering dogs' domesticated dependence on us, it is not unreasonable that anxiety can occur in such a situation. Many rescue dogs that were previously abandoned are predisposed to this anxiety/panic disorder. In such cases, their behavior would appear to be perfectly reasonable and entirely rational. Among dogs that weren't abandoned, those who are coddled and spoiled are prone to separation anxiety. Allowing a dog to be all over its owner is a form of spoiling, as is a dog that does not "work" in some capacity to earn its keep. Work for a companion dog entails going for walks, training, and having something to do (even if that means lying on its bed, like Maya) in enough circumstances where the dog feels it has a function. That said, the major culprit in separation anxiety is owners who constantly coddle their dogs, and we've all seen them. The dogs are constantly in their owner's lap and follow them everywhere. The owner often finds this cute and equates this behavior with love. It's not. It is a dog feeling unsafe and worried. This behavior only worsens with time.

Separation anxiety is torturous for the animal experiencing the problem, and conscientious owners can be held hostage by it. Neighbors will be privy to constant barking and howling when the dog's owner runs to the grocery store. Behaviors range from moderate whining and barking to excessive barking and crying that literally does not stop. When left alone for too long, dogs will often injure themselves and destroy the household. I've seen dogs destroy their teeth by attempting to chew their way out of metal crates. I even worked with a dog that jumped out of a second-story window. They also soil their environments and take on all sorts of compulsive behaviors in an effort to distract themselves from the emotional discomfort.

Separation anxiety can be cured. Dogs can learn a sense of independence and security as well as they can learn commands. Predictably, it begins with the dog being left alone in very small doses and building time as you go. The greatest challenge often lies with the owner who has confused a dog's hyper-dependence with love. It is sometimes very difficult for a person to let go of a dog for any stretch of time. In some cases, separation anxiety exposes the codependent nature of the owner, as loving a dog is always safe. In these cases, it is especially important to remember that the dog feels unduly burdened and is in a perpetual state of panic. To love a dog is to allow it a measure of independence.

Treatment

Always exercise the dog before you leave the house, for two reasons: 1) to bring down energy levels; and 2) the dog will need to be crated or gated, and at first this may feel confining. Exercise will allow the dog to associate coming home with resting and unwinding.

Crate/Gate Training

It will be necessary to crate or gate the dog in a small room. (Crate/ gate training is described in Chapter 10, "Tips, Tools, and Tidbits.")

Desensitization

A dog must be able to occupy itself and cope with being alone. In desensitizing and reconditioning, the initial exposure to being alone should be short and successful before time is added.

To begin: with the dog crated or behind a gate, walk around while still in view. When you go out of sight, make a phone call so the dog can hear your voice.

From there, quietly go in and out of a room just beyond the dog's view. Progress to walking out of the door for less than a minute. As the dog's confidence builds, you can add time accordingly. Build with blocks of five to ten minutes and work up to an hour.

It is advisable to take advantage of weekends so you can train throughout the day. There is no such thing as a saturation point in working on separation anxiety—for the dog, anyway. When I've worked with extreme cases, I will take the dog out for a ten-minute walk every hour, followed by crating, and then have the owners leave for ten minutes.

Cheat

Always have a rotation of special chews and frozen treats when crating the dog.

The "stay" command is effective for working with a dog that is already triggered. It is necessary to show the dog that it's safe to be apart, even if it is just a few feet. Preferably, the dog should stay on a dog bed, in a crate, or in a gated area when the initial separation occurs. Offering a chew stick will keep the dog occupied. Remember, draw on your patience and be disciplined enough to ignore any protestations.

A dog with separation anxiety must not be allowed to sleep in its owner's bed, with no exceptions. Even if the dog panics when kept in a separate room, the transition can begin by crating the dog in the bedroom before moving it just outside the bedroom door and eventually into another room. Try placing a gate in the bedroom doorway and putting the dog bed on the other side so the dog can retain line of sight.

In many cases, a dog's anxiety levels will rise when it sees its people readying to leave the house. Watching you get dressed, grab your keys, and take purposeful strides toward the door can panic a dog. To desensitize the dog, simply perform some of these activities and don't leave. When actually leaving, pretend you hate long goodbyes, since big and extended departures only add to the anxiety. Just leave without fanfare and try not to look back. The same principles hold true upon returning. Do not make a show of it. The goal is to communicate that comings and goings are no big deal.

Another ticket out of the hell of separation anxiety is socialization. Exposing a dog to other people and other dogs expands its world. This experience can have a profound impact on its well-being. I suggest hiring a dog walker who will take the dog out with a pack, and try to convince friends and family to take the dog for a walk.

In my travels I've noticed that people working from home often end up with dogs that have separation anxiety. It is essential for these people to get needed time apart from their best friend. Building relationships with fellow dog owners and tending to each other's dogs is great for dogs and helps owners manage their schedules better. Hitting the dog park allows dogs to explore the world away from their owner, even while the owner is present. It may require a gentle nudge to get your dog to mingle, so be prepared to initiate the socializing by playing with other dogs if yours is behaving like a "cling-on."

Separation anxiety has become pandemic in this country, and the solution is largely common sense. While dogs are supportive they should not be our support systems.

AGGRESSION/TERRITORIAL BEHAVIOR

Warning

I do not wish to directly advise anyone with a dog that has been genuinely aggressive toward people. I can say that these dogs are not hopeless, but without being able to physically see the dog, I cannot in good conscience provide much guidance. I strongly encourage those individuals to contact a professional. I have worked with many aggressive dogs that have gone on to have full lives without incident. I emphatically suggest researching a trainer who has proven success with this issue.

For the sake of this writing, I am equating aggression and territorial behavior with strong reactivity that easily eclipses what I described in the "home reactivity" section.

Some dogs are more reactive than others. It is that simple. Among reactive dogs, aggression is just one of the available options among flight, fight, and freeze. It does not say anything negative about the dog's character.

Common Examples

On- or off-leash aggression, either inside or outside the home, toward dogs, people, small animals, children, and objects—skateboards, vehicles, and the vacuum, of course.

Desensitization

Typically, dogs that have aggressive reactions can be reconditioned through normal exposure as long as they are kept at a safe distance. Use redirection techniques around the triggering stimulus. Pace and patience are everything, so go slowly. For dogs that experience intro-duction aggression, see Chapter 8, "Just to Be Social," and reference the sections "Intros and Outros" and "My Dog Is Trouble."

Tip

Owners have a tendency to heighten the dog's reaction by being nervous. Although it is an understandable response, give calm to get calm, and keep about a foot of slack on the leash. Commands (provided the dog has a sound handle on them) can override some aggressive and territorial tendencies.

Culprits

Lack of socialization and inadequate exercise. Aggression/terri-torial behavior is a learned socialization issue wherein dogs have misunderstood their role, not been properly acclimated to their environment, or reacted in a justifiable way to abuse and violence.

Be aware of environments that are not appropriate for your dog, as some dogs are generally fine but have particular trouble in dog parks or in crowds and similar high-energy places. While I don't normally support outright avoidance, depending on how challenged the dog is, sometimes the simple solution is to avoid these places and situations.

JEALOUS BEHAVIOR

Some dogs will attempt to claim possession of their owners and consider anyone who wishes to spend time with them a threat. It is not uncommon for a dog to dislike a new boyfriend/girlfriend; I've even worked with a few dogs that took a clear side in a marriage. A threatened dog might take on the role of protector and will be reactive toward the exchange of affection between a man and a woman. These behaviors are highly common in dogs with separation anxiety but "jealousy" can be a stand-alone issue.

Symptoms
Constantly rubbing against the owner, sitting too close to the owner, growling or snapping at other people or animals that enter the owner's proxemic space, policing other animals or children in the home, and stealing toys or food. Dogs with jealousy issues are always vying for their owner's attention and often become reactive when their owner shows affection toward another person or animal.

Culprits

Spoiling a dog and insufficient socialization are often the cause, as well as owners who are unaware of the message they are sending in the daily activities with their dog.

Treatment

Setting up boundaries is a key. Have a dog sit/stay in a destination spot with the leash on, and reward even a moment's patience while you show affection or interest in another dog or person. Do not test the dog by becoming exceptionally demonstrative or make baby talk. Add time as you go. Crate/gates may be used. Consistently have the dog spend time with other dogs and people, both separately and together.

Although it may seem small, I've noticed that literally all the people I've worked with who have jealous dogs are terrible walkers. Without exception, they let the dog lead. The dog is the first one out the door, on and off the elevator, and generally walks ahead of the person. Please be mindful of this and try to notice where the dog may be getting the message that it needs to be in the role of guardian.

NOTHING TO FEAR

Confidence is a skill that can be cultivated. I've helped dogs get over issues ranging from aquaphobia to fears of horses, brooms, thunder, and even spoons. The most common misstep people make is attempting to allay the dog's concern by consoling it with kind words and affection. While well-intended, baby talk and conciliatory petting often communicate that the fear is real and the response appropriate.

Desensitizing

An owner's support comes from not sharing in this fear and, as per usual, by confidently but slowly exposing the dog to the trigger.

Generic Fears

Fears of loud vehicles, thunder, and fireworks are common.

Treatment

Using thunder as an example: With the dog on a leash, do not let it run to a hiding place. Maintain a happy attitude and monitor tension levels. Redirect the dog's attention onto some worthwhile treats and attempt to play with the dog. Tug toys, for whatever reason, have worked especially well for me. Have realistic expectations. Some dogs will never be thrilled that the sky is booming and that's okay.

Practice desensitization by cranking up some music while you play with your dog. Bang on a table now and again, and be sure to play with the dog to create a positive association.

Fears of Objects

Skateboards and vacuum cleaners head this list, but it includes any common item that makes its share of noise, such as blenders, lawn mowers, and even running water.

Treatment

Desensitize and redirect: Objects with wheels and noisy appliances can inspire fear in a dog. Desensitize by first exposing the dog to the object while it is not in use. Reward the dog for not reacting, and once it is comfortable around the object, momentarily introduce the triggering sound. Reward again. Build some tolerance to the sound and then walk by the noisy object with your dog. Once the dog is successfully performing a walk-by, try to see if the dog can be comfortable with the sound from a reasonable distance (distance depends on the object; a lawn mower is typically more threatening than a blender) for an extended period of time. Once the dog is more comfortable, use the sit/stay command around the trigger.

Be very generous with rewards when desensitizing. Having top-notch toys at the ready when a vacuum is turned on is a good idea.

Fear of Riding in Cars

Desensitizing

With the car engine off, have the dog get in and out of the vehicle, and be ready with treats or toys. Once this is mastered, get in the car with treats in hand. The dog will likely consider joining you. Once inside, turn the engine on and off a few times before letting the dog out, provided it is not terrified. Lure the dog back into the car with treats, and when the dog hops in, start the car and drive a very short distance. As the dog gains confidence, try a lap around the block and go from there. Close destinations such as dog parks will help create positive associations.

Aquaphobia for Dogs: Fear of Hoses and Faucets

A dog may have a fear of water, but in nearly all cases, hoses, faucets, the sound of loud running water (the shower and drawing a bath), and getting in the bath are what frighten the dog.

Desensitizing

The aim is to get the dog into a dry tub. For this, lure or bribe or manipulate your dog with treats. When the dog is comfortable with being in the tub, run the faucet until there is an inch or two of water. Add water accordingly. Getting a dog used to being in the tub with running water is no small task; frankly, it is a big support job. It is one of those rare instances when coddling, holding, and continually praising the dog actually sends the right message and works effectively.

Tip

Dogs are often more afraid of the faucet than the water. Fill the tub before the dog enters the bathroom. Should you need to run the faucet, have the dog face away from it.

Hoses

An active hose can spook a dog, so turning it on and hunting the dog down is a no-no. Allow the dog to sniff and investigate the hose when it's not running. Introduce the running water slowly, and redirect the dog primarily with toys and secondarily with treats. Once the dog is getting wet, hold him and offer support. It is best to begin by wetting the dog's backside. Before long, this can become a favorite activity.

■ Justin has Pacino inspect this foreign object in order to gain a comfort level.

■ By using treats, Pacino deals with a little gently running water. Note: Justin initially runs the water on Pacino's backside to limit his fear response.

■ Justin supports Pacino as he applies water more liberally.

SENSITIVITY TRAINING

Some dogs are simply touch-sensitive. Many do not take well to being inspected by the vet or brushed by a groomer. Always make sure there is nothing physically wrong that is causing the dog pain.

Cautionary Tale

Miniature poodles have curly hair and not fur, and this coat does not shed. A client of mine used a shedding brush intended to shear shedding fur from short-coated dogs. The brushings were painful, and this dog was now afraid of all brushing.

Redemption Tale

We purchased the appropriate brush and got to work. To desensitize the traumatized poodle, I put her on leash while holding a fistful of treats. I let the dog nibble from my hand as I merely showed her the brush for a few seconds. I then touched her with the smooth backside of the brush as she continued nibbling from my half-closed fistful of small treats. The dog was reactive to a degree, but each session lasted maybe two minutes, with ten-minute breaks until I was able to brush her with the smooth side. In the attempts that followed, I managed a few strokes without the treats. I would say it was a little over an hour before the reactiveness was gone and we were able to easily brush the dog's hair.

Any touch sensitivity that a dog may exhibit can be treated in this fashion so long as one is patient. In many cases, toys will work far better than treats. You need to be ready to experiment.

CHAPTER 10

TIPS, TOOLS, AND TIDBITS

"If there were only a dog here."

—THOMAS A. EDISON (OVERHEARD AT A PARTY)

I decided to include a list of relative miscellany that has varying relevance in the lives of dog owners. As each dog is unique, so is the journey of training and acclimating each animal to its environment and people. While some of these things have been mentioned in previous chapters, forgive the redundancy (this apology is a long time coming, I realize) and allow yourself to record the information in two places.

CRATE/GATE TRAINING

Crates and tension gates offer myriad benefits for dog and puppy owners. They give them their own space, keep unsupervised dogs separated, limit the damage dogs can do around the house, are an excellent tool to treat separation anxiety, aid in housebreaking, and offer a place for dogs to unwind after exercise. The crate/gate is not a cage to lock a dog away; nor should it ever be used as punishment to "ground" your dog. A gate is sometimes preferable if space is an issue, since they can be placed in doorways. Gated areas should be dog-proofed, meaning all hazards are removed.

A crate should provide adequate ventilation, visibility, a soft dog mat, and water to drink. For a dog to acclimate to its crate, begin by placing special chew treats that the dog receives only in the crate. Use treats that would be of high value, such as marrow bones, toys that can be stuffed with peanut butter or turkey, and bully sticks. When you purchase a new dog toy, use the "go to crate" command and give the toy as a reward.

■ Kennedy sits in her crate—a safe haven with a soft bed, water, chew toys, some treats, and play toys. This is about the size of many New York apartments.

To use the crate or gate properly, always have the dog enter after plenty of exercise. A dog's crate is a sanctuary for unwinding, resting, and relaxing. It is not a place to put a dog unattended for hours at a time. A dog's adjustment period will take a couple of weeks, beginning with ten-to-fifteen-minute sessions while the owner is present. Once the dog is crated, owners should go out of sight as they do their business. As time is added, and builds to an hour or more, it is generally safe for an owner to leave without concern. Should a dog whine when an owner leaves the room, try making a phone call so the dog can hear your voice. Place the dog in the crate or gated area whenever he appears sleepy, in order to capture a positive association. As a dog gains comfort in the new space, open and close the door to your home in order to desensitize the dog to the sounds of leaving. It is not uncommon for a dog to be gated or crated overnight. In the case of separation anxiety, keeping the crate in the owner's bedroom is acceptable at first. Since autonomy is the goal for the dog and human, the crate should be transitioned to another room in roughly a week.

With the exception of dogs that are comfortable being crated overnight, I recommend that adult dogs not be crated or gated longer than four hours, and in the case of puppies, two hours. This is not a hard-and-fast rule, as some dogs willingly spend long periods of time in their crates.

WAGS, BITES, AND BARKS

Tail Wagging

While much has been studied on the subject, there are a couple of cues that are commonly misread, particularly the idea that a wagging tail is the sign of a happy dog. While a dog's tail tucked between the legs is a sure sign of submission, depending on the breed, dogs will carry their tails at different heights and wag them at different rates. A tail's height is an indicator of mood. A tail at mid-height means the dog is relaxed, while a high tail is a sign of a dog attempting to threaten and establish dominance. It is not a perfect indicator, as beagles and terriers naturally walk with their tails held high, while greyhounds have naturally low-slung tails. It is necessary to determine the average height that an individual dog holds its tail before determining if the tail is telltale. The speed of the wag lets one know just how excited the dog is. How much the tail swings determines a dog's emotional state. There is a lot to this, and endless combinations, but here are some common tail movements and their meaning:

- A big, wide wag is friendly, not challenging in any way, and is the origin of the "wagging tail means happy dog" stereotype. When the wagging tail is accompanied by swinging hips, that's one happy dog.

- A vibrating tail that moves speedily is a sign that the dog is about to go into fight or flight. If the tail is held high, it is most likely ready to attack.

- A slow-dragging wag with a low or half-slung tail speaks to an insecure dog that is not feeling terribly social or particularly good.

- Small wags at an average speed are humble greetings. The dog is saying, "Hi, are you sure it's okay that I come in?"

In a recent study conducted at the University of Trieste in Italy, a neuroscientist and two veterinarians tracked the angles that a dog's tail would wag. They discovered that dogs feeling positive will wag their tail with a bias to the right side, and when they are experiencing negative feelings, they will wag their tail more to the left. Interesting stuff.

Smiling

Dogs can smile. That happy-looking, partially open mouth accompanied by a slight tilt of the head and relaxed ears is indicative of a good mood.

■ Dexter and Buna crackin' a smile for the camera.

A dog will dive into a play bow (its rear end in the air and its front paws and elbows on the ground) when inviting other dogs to play. In such a circumstance, any barking and growling is playful in nature. For new dog owners, telling the difference between fighting and rambunctious play can be challenging. The play bow can let someone know that all is well.

Barks and Growls

Barking and growling are how dogs talk; these sounds also act as a sophisticated alarm system. A growl can serve as a warning that aggression is on the way, as can offensive barking. Lower-pitched sounds signal the potential for aggression, while higher-pitched sounds are invitations to play. The longer the duration of the bark or growl, the stronger a dog's intent is to act on the bark. Barks and growls that are shorter in frequency indicate the presence of fear. Sounds delivered at a fast rate are signs of excitement and possibly urgency. One or two short barks that are midrange in pitch are a dog's way of saying hello and are commonly heard when the doorbell rings. When a dog dives into the play bow, a short, stuttering bark is the invitation to play. A string of individual barks communicates that a dog is lonely and likely asking for your company. Security dogs will bark low, slow, and continuously to alert others to the presence of an intruder and that danger is coming. The "call of the wild" bark is a string of two to four barks delivered with pauses and is the most common. It is not necessarily a battle cry but a way of calling the gang together because something requires investigation.

I've found there is some signature to a dog's bark and growl once you get to know them. Chiquita has a long, low growl she'll use to rouse me when I'm sleeping. What's this mean? She has to go to the bathroom and in no small way. Pacino is not much of a barker; the only time he really barks is when he's trying to goad another dog into play.

Nipping and Biting

Dogs at play mouth and nip each other's necks and ears, and this is how they learn bite inhibition. Unfortunately, some dogs are slow learners and may play too rough with others. Proper socialization is helpful, but in places like a dog park, it is an owner's responsibility to judge how well a dog gives and takes in order to avoid altercations.

TREATS, CHEWS, AND SNACKS

Always check with a vet, or do some research to determine which foods are healthiest for your dog. I recommend treats that will occupy dogs for as long as possible when they are at home. Treats like chew sticks are designed to be long lasting, while edibles such as raw marrow bones, peanut butter, wet dog food, and even cold cuts can be frozen.

I strongly advocate the use of rubber toys with hollow centers that can be filled with food. They come in different sizes and textures to accommodate different strengths of jaws and teeth. Dogs were made to hunt and scavenge for their food, and having to work to get the food out of these puzzle toys gives dogs a chance to perform one of nature's designed purposes. A dog will lick, paw, nibble, and roll the toy around in order to release the food. This practice provides a dog with purpose and helps to defeat boredom and anxiety. Frozen treats are more time-consuming, while moist food is pretty easy for a dog to get to. Frozen treats are great for crate training, as they do wonders to keep a dog occupied while adjusting to the new space.

Marrow Bones

Raw, never cooked. I get them at the butcher and store them in the freezer. The hard texture of the bone helps rub plaque off teeth, though for dogs with sensitive teeth, it can chafe the enamel or chip teeth, so consult a vet before using. The marrow is rich in healthy fats and nutrients but can be difficult for certain dogs to digest and is never recommended for puppies.

General Treats

I use treats primarily when training dogs and prefer them to be of the small, soft, and bite-sized variety so the reward can be consumed quickly. Treats on shelves can be hit or miss, so do your research, or try some of my personal favorites: Sliced turkey, baby carrots, cooked broccoli stems, and low-fat string cheese are all of high nutritional value and work very well.

TOOLS OF THE TRADE

Leashes

I prefer four- to six-foot nylon leads for walking. Longer leads make it more challenging to control the dog, and the intimate communication with the leash is lost. In populous areas, I also feel it is a basic responsibility not to have dogs wandering on a long leash. Even though I use a shorter lead, I will tie a knot approximately two feet

■ The proper way to hold a four-foot leash. Justin likes to tie a knot in the right spot where he has control and the dog still has a little slack.

from the collar clip for a better hold while still providing some comfortable slack. For teaching the "stay" command outdoors, nothing beats a long training leash, which can be as long as thirty feet.

Martingale Collars

Also known as the greyhound or whippet collar, these collars were originally designed for greyhounds because their necks are larger than their heads and can often slip out of traditional side-release collars. These collars have gained in popularity across all breeds for being humane, as they limit the amount of pressure that can be applied and hang loosely when they are not being pulled. They are great to use both in training and on a daily basis, particularly for dogs prone to pulling.

Head Halter Collars

See Chapter 9, "Living in the Solution," and reference the section "Pulling/Halting on Leash" for a detailed description. Head halters are excellent for high-energy, pulling, and reactive dogs. The collar is effective in redirecting a reactive dog because it leads the dog by the muzzle.

Harnesses

Although I'm not a big proponent of harnesses, they do have their application with dogs under ten pounds in weight and dogs with trachea issues. I much prefer harnesses where the leash clips around the dog's chest as opposed to those that clip to the upper back.

There are dozens of tools for training dogs. Extension leashes, prong collars, remote collars, clickers, among the full suite of products that are offered everywhere. I typically don't endorse or oppose any tool so long as it's used properly and humanely. I've noticed some of the newer products have a bit of a learning curve, so be sure to have a handle on how they work before use. All dogs learn and respond differently and owners will find that some things work better for them than others. Remember, it's the owner and her technique, not the tool, that does the training.

CHAPTER 11

PUTTING IT ALL TOGETHER

"Properly trained, a man can be a dog's best friend."

—COREY FORD

Now that you've learned to speak some dog, it's time to put this newfound knowledge to good use. In order to become the best dog owner you can be, you must take what you've learned and incorporate it into a daily practice. The goal is to provide a fulfilling lifestyle that will meet your dog's needs for exercise, socialization, structure, love, and health. Let's lay out a "perfect world" plan that we can all try to adhere to. Though we may fall short from time to time, the dog will forgive us for being human.

To keep a dog physically and mentally fit, it is an absolute must that the owner and dog go for walks together. This is one of the jobs that a companion dog performs in order to get a sense of well-being. Dogs require a bare minimum of one hour of walking a day, with one and a half hours or more being the goal. Walks consist of relief walks and exercise/play walks that can be broken up to meet both the owner's and dog's needs. Typically, two to three fifteen-minute relief walks are the norm to go with one long exercise walk of an hour or more, or two exercise walks that are at least thirty minutes long. Relief walks can be more lightly supervised than exercise walks. When my dogs need to do their business, I don't sweat minor misbehaving and occasionally poor manners.

Exercise walks should involve active participation with a dog dad or mom who will maintain a brisk pace, keep an eye on the pooch, and be as interactive as possible. Bring a ball, and have the dog carry a stick. Periodically perform some commands (such as the heeling technique) to bolster the dog's sense of canine purpose. Keep treats with you to reward the dog, and always remember that having a backyard may allow the dog some extra activity but does not replace the purposeful and intimate time shared on walks.

With respect to weather and walking, it is largely dependent upon breed and a dog's coat. For short-haired and smaller dogs, temperatures below freezing can warrant a dog jacket, and snow can freeze on a dog's paws, cracking and damaging skin. Some things to avoid outright are the chemicals and salts placed on the road and sidewalks to melt ice. These are painful, erode the pads on a dog's paw, and toxic should a dog ingest them when licking himself clean. In these circumstances, snowshoes and waxes can provide needed protection. The wax solution should always be wiped off after the walk.

The rain is certainly harmless, though some dogs are highly averse to feeling raindrops falling on their head, while others are more bothered by raincoats than the rain. This is a personal call, and the dog's preference will not take long to find out.

The heat is something to be wary of. Dogs are susceptible to sunburn, and they can overheat pretty quickly. Scalding sidewalks can burn their paws and it's hard to miss a dog hopping on the sidewalk in discomfort. Always walk your dog on the shady side of a street, and do your best to keep his paws wet. Bring plenty of water to keep everyone hydrated, including you.

As for the accessories, I'll again plug the four-foot leash, since its relatively short length allows for better communication. A good walking chemistry is always interactive, and the leash acts as the artery of communication. The right collar also makes a difference; I much prefer martingale-style collars, because harnesses are impersonal and tend to hoist the dog. More on martingale collars can be found in Chapter 10, "Tips, Tools, and Tidbits."

Prior to going on exercise walks, make sure the dog shows good manners by remaining seated when the leash is put on. He should also exhibit a calm disposition before leaving the home. This sets the tone for the walk. That said, I offer a little leeway by giving my dogs the freedom to sniff, explore, and do their business when we first get out the door.

Once a dog's need for purposeful exercise is met, dogs are always psyched to socialize with other dogs and people. Dog parks can be hit or miss, but there are plenty to choose from, so finding a "sweet spot" is just a matter of trial and error. I suggest everyone try a few and revisit the second and third favorites from time to time to keep things fresh. Typically, the same people and dogs can be seen at the park around the same times. It is only natural that you and your dog will have better chemistry in some parks versus others. Once a dog has made friends with a few dogs at the park, be bold and ask to set up a playdate. Knowing fellow dog owners can alleviate some of the responsibility that comes with caring for a dog. Should dog parks prove disappointing, pack walks can fill the void in a dog's social life. Walking a few dogs together creates a unified sense of drive and purpose between dogs and can help a dog overcome smaller issues, like halting. Once a dog owner and a few dogs get to know one another, walking them together gets easier and easier.

Since training is an ongoing process, incorporate short sessions at the park to reinforce and prove a dog's knowledge of commands. Work on the "come," "sit," and "stay" commands (or any others that need further proofing) in the park. Any dog that can follow commands in the company of other dogs off leash and at play is well trained.

There is a correct protocol to entering and leaving a dog park, which is to have your dog sit/stay before you open the gate. Always make sure no one is coming or going when you are, because leashes get tangled and dog scuffles can take place in very tight quarters. Once the coast is clear, enter and turn the dog loose, but don't be the person whose head is in her phone or texting while her dog runs amuck. Walk around, greet other dogs and people (if you're up to it), and take in the action. Some of the most calming times for me have come through watching groups of dogs at play.

Believing one is finished with training a dog is tantamount to being finished with learning as a person. When refining the basic commands, maintaining specific skills, or ironing out the kinks of a lingering issue, it's worthwhile to schedule a fifteen-to-thirty-minute session into the day. The best times are mealtimes, so the dog can earn its dinner, or after exercise, when the dog's energy has been somewhat depleted. General maintenance of a dog's repertoire can be worked in as the opportunity presents itself. Every dog will provide its owner with daily opportunities for training. For example, when giving your dog a new play toy, have the dog perform any combination of commands before it runs off to play. A dog that remains on a training maintenance plan keeps the knives sharp, and these knives cut out a lot of potential problems. Should things get mundane, look up a trick or a complex command and work on teaching that to your dog. Outside of exercise walks, training is where our bond truly flourishes.

Now that the dog has been taken out, exercised, trained, and enjoyed some structured play, he should be a pleasure in the home. That may sound ambitious to some, but a well-trained and exercised dog must be able to relax on his own and give his owners space when needed. A dog's energy level inside the home should be relatively easy to moderate. A dog will need a few toys to play with, treats and chew toys to gnaw on, and periodic play sessions. Toys lose their value quickly, so leave only a few out at a time in order to retain some novelty; buy new ones when the old ones start to feel lackluster.

What is an acceptable level of playing in the house is a personal choice. Personally, I love playing tug-of-war with rope toys in my apartment because there is no major movement involved and I can do it sitting down or standing up. Being able to successfully allow your dogs to get riled up indoors is a matter of being able to control a dog's energy levels. A firm knowledge of "drop it," "go to (bed, crate, spot)," and "stay" are required. When a dog can perform these commands in the heat of play, that means it is able to access its internal calming switch, which is a sign of good training. Feel free to pat yourself on the back.

Nothing provides a sense of calm and well-being like being on the receiving end of affection. A good dog owner knows how to let the dog spend appropriate time curled up by her side and is also aware of the dog that gloms on and "loves too much." A constant need for affection is often a precursor to separation anxiety, so affection should be doled out responsibly and on your terms. Responsible owners dedicate time for themselves and practice quality separation with the sit/stay/go to your spot commands or by using a crate or gate. Have a designated spot for your dog when you're eating and always be aware that a dog is best occupied when it has a place to go and/or an activity it is supposed to be doing.

The rules of the roost are clear, and when they are not, there is a protocol that dictates. In my house, my dogs are allowed up on the couch or in my bed when they are invited, and prior to this they must be relaxed. Chilling out is a lot more fun for everybody when the dogs are chill.

When it comes to food, puppies eat three to four times per day, while adult dogs get fed twice; exercising portion control is vital. We should also offer some food or treats by hand every day. Dogs should be fed after exercise, as if offering a bounty for a successful hunt. A dog should exhibit calm before being fed and should be sitting in a designated spot while the food is being prepared. When placing the food bowl in front of the dog, have him wait for a moment before releasing him to eat. Occasionally practice desensitization by placing treats in his bowl while he's eating, and feel free to use the "drop it" command with chewable treats to ward off food aggression.

In order to maintain a dog's general health, you must implement a sound practice of brushing and grooming. Dogs need to have their teeth brushed a couple of times a week, while a proper bath, depend-